Superhuman Innovation

Transforming business with artificial intelligence

Chris Duffey

Kogan Page
INSPIRE

Publisher's note
Every possible effort has been made to ensure that the information contained in this book is accurate at the time of going to press, and the publisher and author cannot accept responsibility for any errors or omissions, however caused. No responsibility for loss or damage occasioned to any person acting, or refraining from action, as a result of the material in this publication can be accepted by the editor, the publisher or the author.

First published in Great Britain and the United States in 2019 by Kogan Page Limited

2nd Floor, 45 Gee Street	122 W 27th St, 10th Floor	4737/23 Ansari Road
London	New York, NY 10001	Daryaganj
EC1V 3RS	USA	New Delhi 110002
United Kingdom		India

© Chris Duffey 2019

The right of Chris Duffey to be identified as the author of this work has been asserted by him in accordance with the Copyright, Designs and Patents Act 1988.

Chart design by Connor Delaney

Chapter opening graphics from Adobe Stock

ISBNs

Hardback   978 0 7494 9804 7
Paperback   978 0 7494 8383 8
eBook   978 0 7494 8384 5

British Library Cataloguing-in-Publication Data

A CIP record for this book is available from the British Library.

Library of Congress Cataloging-in-Publication Data

A CIP record for this book is available from the Library of Congress.

Typeset by Integra Software Services, Pondicherry
Print production managed by Jellyfish
Printed and bound in Great Britain by CPI Group (UK) Ltd, Croydon CR0 4YY

To my parents, who instilled in me the love of life-long learning

To my wife and two daughters, who are my constant inspiration

To my sister, who showed me what honest success looks like

Contents

CONTENTS

About the author

Chris Duffey spearheads Adobe's Creative Cloud strategic development innovation partnerships across the creative enterprise space.

Chris and his work have been profiled by *The Wall Street Journal, The Guardian, Inc., Adweek, Adage, Cheddar, The Mirror, The Drum, Campaign*, CMO.com, *NYPost, Business Insider*, and have been featured by Google, McKinsey and Wharton in their digital marketing book. Chris also serves on Rutgers University Data Advisory Board and the Board of Directors for ANA NY.

Prior to Adobe Chris was an award-winning executive creative director, speaker, author and AI and mobile technologist. *Business Insider* named him as one of 'the industry's leaders on the top issues, challenges and opportunities in the fast-changing world of mobile marketing'. He has been a creative consultant with 35 advertising agencies across all the major global holding companies: WPP, IPG, Havas, Omnicom, Publicis and MDC, and has worked across every major industry vertical. Chris is an accomplished author on the inevitable relevance of AI and mobile, with an affinity towards creating innovation for the most complex business challenges imaginable. *The Guardian* listed 'How mobile became mighty in healthcare', an article he co-wrote, in their top ten best healthcare stories of the year.

Chris's keynotes have received more than 50 million impressions. His sessions have been reported around the world by *Access Hollywood, Extra, OK* magazine, *Hello, People*, the *Daily Mail, NYPost, Adweek* and *The Drum*.

How I used artificial intelligence to write this book

Throughout my career as a creative director and creative tech-nologist, I have always been fascinated when human creativity and ingenuity meet and is then amplified by technology. We will explore in great depth in the upcoming pages how, over the past number of years, artificial intelligence has become one of the great-est technical advances. I wanted to celebrate the capabilities and possibilities of AI, but also to test its limits, not only by writing a book about it but actually using AI to help write it. Capturing AI's current and future abilities has been a journey of exploration which has led to a number of exciting discoveries. But there were also times when it became clear that in some instances AI was just not there yet. So, in the hope of showing how transformational AI can be, I assembled some AI technologies to become a 'co-author'. What follows is an overview of my approach. Much like the writing process, my use of AI was organic and non-linear and often deployed a layering of different techniques.

In the early to mid-2000s we were in a similar new era of mobile. Clients often asked us to describe how a mobile respon-sive website or app was built. Before answering, the first thing was always to decide how many technical layers to peel back: what went into the visual design process, which UX tools were used, an explanation of software development codes, how to use iPhone or Android hardware capabilities and components such as chips, geolocation abilities. The list went on and on. Most recently this was done through full-day tech sessions with the introduction of the Apple Watch and health kit and Amazon Alexa. And, as in the early days of mobile and wearables, we are going through a similar conversation with the technical build-ing blocks of AI. This lays the AI foundation for strategic and creative discussions on how, when and where to make best use of the technology.

Rather than starting out with how is it built or trying to use a specific AI technique, my general approach in using AI as a co-creation tool for this book was to begin with a fundamental question: what can this specific AI function do and how can it help? With this focus I used a number of AI APIs (application program interfaces) while writing. Although they made for a lengthy list, it included everything – from using AI to compose responses on specified topics, the suggestion and prediction of contextual content that might be relevant, translation of multi-language reference materials and then summarization, sentence analysis and separation, constituency parsing to determine sentence structure and meaning, tone analyser to understand emotions and communication style in the text review stage, sentiment analysis to analyse and generate a summary of insights, characteristics and values inherent to the text. In the context of this book, the AI function – or Aimé – is not a single sourced technology but rather a suite of technologies, many of which are open-source, each building on a different set of concepts, approaches and infrastructures. The conversational agent leverages a number of expert systems using AI and ML techniques such as natural language processing (NLP), natural language understanding (NLU) and natural language generation (NLG) APIs. These techniques for example allow Aimé to identify, understand and respond to key words, phrases, ideas and requests, and at times instances of recognition and understanding of experiences and reasoning.

The underlying aspects of the AI used in *Superhuman Innovation* primarily embody three systems: AI voice recognition, AI content understanding and summarization, AI content creation and generation. Voice recognition and continuous dictation enables human-to-system interaction through a voice-user interface (VUI) for tasks such as speech-to-text, text-to-speech, voice editing, formatting, spelling, and sharing documents. AI content understanding and summarization technology reviews and abridges databases, articles or research papers into quick digestible content through approaches such as sentiment analysis, labelling and the organization of higher-level concepts based on contextual understanding. AI content creation and generation is the ability of the system to develop concepts and ideas to aid the content creation process. Writing algorithms to emulating the human writing process helped contribute ideas, titles, content and drafts.

At the risk of getting a bit technical: from a high-level technical architecture standpoint many of the APIs were stationed in cloud environments – meaning they could be accessed via provisioned instances or applications. The algorithms were then called on for functions such as generation, creation, summarization, and content enrichment by being pointed to and accessing research and content databases. Layering a series of APIs allowed for a more comprehensive output. This 'multi-engine' approach is a reflection of a broader AI engineering mindset that focuses on the objective rather than the AI technique or technology. AI development should not be about a specific approach or technology, but putting the human first instead.

The use of AI technology specifically within higher-level tasks like human creativity may be a provocative notion, but AI can enhance innovation and originality. As a reflection of this interactive conversation with AI about AI, *Superhuman Innovation* is written in a dialogue format to demonstrate how AI can achieve the seemingly impossible by leveraging technology to solve problems that we can't solve by ourselves or to help solve them faster.

For those of you who want to spend less time on tedious tasks and more doing what you love doing – this book is for you. For all of you who want to work smarter in order to be more efficient – this book is for you. For anybody of any age, with any skill level – this book is for you. For those of you who want to be more successful – this book is for you. AI is the great democratizer in helping you achieve your goals.

Please read the book to the end. Yes, a section or two may be a bit technical, but let me assure you this is not about the technology; this is about you and what you can achieve with it. If you do make the commitment and make it to the end, you will leave with actionable and tangible opportunities for your business, no matter the size or stage, as well as for your own career management and advancement.

Preface

As a young boy growing up in Milwaukee I had a pet pigeon. Make no mistake about it, Roxanne was not an ordinary pigeon; she was a champion racing pigeon. She was a beautiful pure-bred blue check hen. Band number 2803 – that band is of great significance, as you'll soon see.

I was always amazed at how she and her fellow racing pigeons could find their way home. Every weekend during racing season a special pigeon truck would drive the pigeons to a location hundreds of miles away. The pigeons were released at the exact same moment, starting the race. Even if you're not a fan of pigeons, it's an impressive sight to see. All these winged thoroughbreds blasting out of the gates much like the Kentucky Derby or the Grand National.

My father drove to the race with Roxanne. I waited at home, wondering how in the world could she find her way back from that huge distance. And, thinking about it, along the way she would potentially encounter thunderstorms, survive a suspected hawk attack, dodge aeroplanes and get past any number of other obstacles, but nonetheless she always made it back home.

What is the significance of the band? Each racing pigeon wore a band on their ankle. There was more to the race than just the fact that the pigeon made their way home. Once they arrived, it was my job to get that band and timestamp it. This was done with a special device that looked like an old credit card imprinter.

Once the pigeon arrived that's where I had to get a bit creative. The job was to figure out how to grab the pigeon and take off the band. This step was where the race could be won or lost.

I knew that Roxanne enjoyed a special mix of popcorn seeds – that was our competitive edge in getting her to land and distract her for a split second. She had to be distracted so I could grab that band from her ankle. After that, my Dad and I would race down to the pigeon club and go through a mathematical algorithm calculating the end destination versus time. From the results, the winner would be determined. For a kid growing up in Wisconsin this was competitive sport at its best!

Look at the beak of a pigeon when you get a chance, and you'll notice a little white cluster. It's unusually high in iron. Scientists believe this cluster creates an interaction with the electromagnetic field of the earth, and that serves as the pigeon's internal compass. Pigeons are extraordinary and are unheralded within the animal kingdom. They are phenomenal creatures that can fly 20 miles in minutes, achieve speeds up to 92 mph, fly 700 miles in one day, have eyes that can spot objects up to 26 miles away and have been recorded as flying 7,000 miles in 55 days.

In the 8th century BC, pigeons were used regularly by the Greeks to carry messages about the results of the Olympic games, battles and other events to the various city-states. As impractical as the use of pigeons to relay messages may sound, runners could take days to spread the word. In fact, according to Greek legend it took a whole day for the news of the Persian defeat at Marathon to reach Athens. Just 26 miles, but the runner reputedly died from exhaustion and heat stroke when he arrived. But using a pigeon to deliver the messages only took a few hours.

You may be wondering why we are talking about pigeons in a book about artificial intelligence. It demonstrates that, from early in history, humans used other intelligences to enhance their own natural abilities. The domestication of animals allowed early societies to take advantage of the physical and mental attributes of other beings. Today, computers, and specifically artificial intelligence, are expanding our abilities into the 'superhuman' range.

We harness computers in much the same way as we did with animals, to perform tasks that complement or expand our native capabilities or perform work that is repetitious, dangerous or laborious. This is the fundamental premise on how artificial intelligence will amplify human ability into *superhuman innovation* to transform businesses, society and individuals.

Throughout history, the greatest innovators have combined the art of creativity with the logic of science for transformation. Look at Leonardo da Vinci, who considered himself just as much of a man of science and technology as an artist. It is with this in mind that we'll look at the way in which artificial intelligence (AI) is a convergence of art and science. There is no dispute that AI will have a dramatic impact on the future of business and society, but there is uncertainty on how to apply it.

AI is sometimes referred to as the new electricity of our time. It is revolutionizing industries the world over and is changing how we fundamentally view and understand work. In *Superhuman Innovation* I'll show you how AI will supercharge the workforce and world of work and how it can be harnessed to deliver powerful change to how companies innovate and gain competitive advantage. The book is a practical guide that explains how AI and machine learning are impacting not only the way businesses, brands and people innovate, but also *what* they innovate with their products, services and content.

Introduction

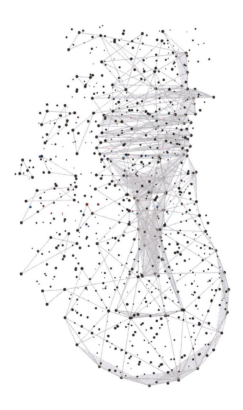

The second mind

Something wondrous happens in early childhood around the age of two. This is when children develop the understanding that other people have their own thoughts and feelings, in other words, the theory of the second mind. This theory describes the ability of individuals to understand that others have beliefs, intents, desires, emotions that are different from theirs. Humanity is now having a moment of awakening much like this, where we are now realizing the theory of the second mind with artificial intelligence. Artificial intelligence (AI), the 'second mind', will expand and propel our abilities and intelligence beyond what we ever imagined.[1]

What if we could tap into superhuman powers to be better at school, excel at sports, succeed in business and ultimately live a longer and fuller life? Who wouldn't want that competitive edge? With this inspiration in mind, this book unpacks the magic around the possibilities of AI, demystifies AI into practical strategies and provides a mindset to apply AI to business innovation and transformation.

The superhuman framework centres on the five key tenets of AI: *speed*, *understanding*, *performance*, *experimentation* and *results*. We will discuss, analyse and debate these in the forthcoming pages.

As a father, husband, son and brother, and holding down a full-time dream job at Adobe, my days are packed – much like many of you – and the thought of writing a book was a sizeable challenge. However, in the pursuit of 'walking the walk' I've leveraged AI to help co-author much of the narrative in the following pages. In doing so I dramatically reduced the time taken to create this book. As a metaphor for how AI is giving us superhuman powers, and for the purposes of this book, we have given AI a name: Aimé, which is derived from the French for 'beloved' (*bien aimé*) and is also coincidentally a combination of AI + me. Aimé reflects the goal of this book – to show

3

that AI will become your beloved co-creator and your intelligent personal assistant going forward.

Aimé illustrates the role and relationship that humanity is now starting to have with AI. Much like Amazon Alexa, bots, Siri and other voice assistants we are moving into an age of intelligent assistants, where they will be companions that predict our needs, inspire, amplify our human abilities and enhance our evolutionary state of being. Throughout the book, Aimé learns from me, aids my thoughts, suggests and interprets my needs, contributes humour to situations. This is reflective of where advancements are being made in 'narrow AI'.

The future has no patience with the timid, so let's not waste any time and get straight into *Superhuman Innovation: Transforming business with artificial intelligence*. As a hint of what's to come, here is a verbal narrative trailer. The conversation is divided into three parts: the AI foundation; the AI activation; and the AI future.

Part 1: The AI foundation

Greetings from the future of innovation. Every 10 to 15 years the world receives a new game-changing technology platform. Look at what the desktop computing and publishing revolution achieved for the democratization of the creation of and access to information via the internet. This was soon followed by the ubiquity of mobile devices that helped deliver all this content. That vast amount of data created the need for cloud storage. The desire to take advantage of that information, or digital exhaust (data that is the result of the choices and actions made by people online)[2] led to the acceleration of the development of AI.

In other words, artificial intelligence, in many ways, was driven by the need for a tool to make sense of all this data.

Because of its potential, AI has been compared to the invention of electricity, as an ambient operating system that will light the future way for business innovation. AI has the potential to innovate the creation of products, services and experiences at scale and will then power automation to increase productivity for these outputs. Innovators have always been in the business of creating opportunities for their products and customers, and AI supercharges that opportunity.

There's a saying (attributed to Albert Einstein) that the true sign of intelligence is not knowledge but imagination; this is one of the major themes conveyed in this book. In the case of AI, the true measure of intelligence is intelligent imagination. What we mean by that is imagination can now be more informed and more tangibly enlightened through the unlocking of data.

Artificial intelligence is the platform of our time, the medium of the moment that leads us to another goal of this book, the realization that businesses must triple down on the AI value exchange to enhance innovation, because we're at a point in time where AI is finally actionable.

Through the exploration of AI in this book, we'll discover that technology is not good or bad. AI is simply a tool; that's how it is intended to be used. Ultimately, we will not talk about the trend of AI, but rather how to enable this trend to create innovation with relevant, personalized and magical experiences across all industries, societies and cultures.

To put AI's relevance into perspective, if you look across the current cultural landscape you can see AI is permeating everything. Take Hollywood shows and films like *Westworld* and *Morgan*. *Westworld* is about an AI-driven theme park with autonomous robots playing the main characters. *Morgan*, a feature film, is compelling not only because of its AI theme, but also because AI was used to create the movie trailer.

Consider the seminal AI writing of Ray Kurzweil in *How to Create a Mind*, which captured the modern-day and future abilities of AI, as well as the rise of AI voice assistants like Amazon's Alexa and Apple's voice assistant Apple Homepod. Additionally, there is the influx of AI technologies such as Mobileye, used for autonomous cars, which will be discussed in more detail in this book.[3]

Chapter 1 – Changing landscape: Customer behaviours and expectations

To understand better the tremendous opportunities surrounding AI we first must look at the changing landscape. We are living in an unprecedented time of societal transformation. Digital is disrupting every industry, all societies and each individual. Content is being consumed through more devices at a faster rate than ever before. People expect their experiences to be personalized, connected and flawless across every touch point and they won't tolerate anything less: this is what is at the core of the digital transformation. Businesses are now realizing the need to shift from a product-focused approach to an experience focused strategy for both their customers and within their organizations.

Chapter 2 – The digital transformation: From messaging to experiences

Exceptional experiences have become critical to attracting and retaining customers. Creating amazing and inspirational content is key. Powerful experiences change the way we interact, entertain, work and relate to the world around us. Experiences can be one-on-one, among families, friends, co-workers, collaborative, or through engaging in social media. They can also be one-to-many, business-to-consumer, business-to-business, teacher-to-student, government-to-citizen, artist-to-audience, and so on. Today, these data-informed experiences are how we can break through the noise and make a connection and an impact.

Chapter 3 – Infinite data: Driving better outcomes

Experiences are powered by data and that in turn drives innovative business success. By leveraging the power of data, we can create experiences that matter. For instance, 2.5 quintillion bytes of data are created daily; AI can use much of that data to intelligently determine how consumers are interacting with or abandoning a brand. This helps inform what works and what doesn't, leading to future experiences improved by insights, supported by data and brought to life through beautiful, powerful created experiences.[4]

However, AI is not about the technology in or of itself; it's about how technology can be leveraged to assist in creating these immersive and unexpected experiences. With AI, machine learning and deep learning systems, machines are becoming indispensable and moving into the realm of superhuman innovation.

Chapter 4 – Infrastructure: The need for a foundation

As with any new technology, the technical and organizational foundation must be in place to realize AI's full potential and value. You can think of infrastructure as five layers:

1 The network
2 Your hardware, such as services and disc drives
3 The data model
4 Databases
5 Applications

On top of all that, you place AI.

Technology must be future-proofed. Scalable. Highly available. Redundant. Disaster recoverable. High-performing. Virtualized. Pick your database wisely to scale well.

Part 2: The AI activation

Chapter 5 – Artificial intelligence: The what and why of the AI revolution

Until the 1980s, schools taught the technical aspects of computing. Fast-forward to today and the methodology is no longer about the technology, but rather it's about putting the computer or the software into action, whether it be handing out iPads to learn maths strategies or using a smartboard for reading.

With that in mind, we're at a similar point with artificial intelligence. We don't start off with the technical aspects but instead we focus on how and where it can be used and leveraged to solve business problems. A great metaphor is that of the maestro or the composer. They understand the capabilities of the instruments within their orchestra, but they don't necessarily need to be able to play each of them or know how the instruments were created or constructed. Their role is to bring all those instruments together to create a masterpiece.

That is essentially what we're talking about with artificial intelligence on a business strategy level. Customers and consumers are not interested in the technicalities of AI. They want to know what it can achieve and how AI technology can serve people and businesses.

Chapter 6 – The SUPER framework: A superhuman strategy

In a world of product and pricing parity, the delivery of superior experience of service has become the new marketing and competitive edge. With AI, companies can harness the power of data, personalization and on-demand availability, to name but a few, at the touch of an intelligent button.

This chapter unearths a powerful five-pronged model centring around the acronym SUPER, which describes how AI enables innovation through the offerings of

Speed (by facilitating work processes)
Understanding (by revealing and mastering deep insights)
Performance (by enabling customization of delivery to customers)
Experimentation (by allowing the iterative process of re-invention and feedback)
Results (by providing tangible, measurable and optimizable results)

Chapter 7 – Speed: Facilitating work processes

AI will help with business efficiencies: everything from speed of manufacturing to ideation to content creation to internal processes. For the consumer, this will result in faster service and faster delivery of products.

Chapter 8 – Understanding: Revealing and mastering deep insights

Artificial intelligence will permeate innovation across ideation, campaigns, service bots, applications, attribution and delivery. This chapter showcases examples of how AI makes experiences more effective through better understanding.

Chapter 9 – Performance: Measurement and optimization

As the volume of data and content explodes, companies need to deeply embrace AI and machine learning techniques to unlock true insights from these datasets at scale. With AI/machine learning, cloud computing will evolve from a simple automation layer to an indispensable and pervasive intelligent fabric across organizations for predictive audience segments and hyper-personalization capabilities.

Chapter 10 – Experimentation: Actionable curiosity

We are now at a point in time that is reminiscent of the mid-1990s, where the early winners of the internet were those who identified opportunities and experimented to address those business problems. We are in a very similar setting with AI today. However, there needs to be a systematic game plan for experimentation with AI.

Chapter 11 – Results: Business transformation

As AI matures, we'll be able to measure results in a more quantifiable way because AI can quickly process vast volumes of data and make inferences based on what it finds. This opens up the power of predictive analytics and highlights the value of the virtuous feedback loop.

Part 3: The AI future

Chapter 12 – Where to start

The first question to answer when beginning an AI project is to figure out where to start. Before beginning, define the problem to be solved and who needs the solution. Put the customer first beyond all else.

Chapter 13 – Security, privacy and ethics

There are two sides to AI in security. First, AI must be secure, and that introduces challenges. Second, AI can be used to improve security, solving one of the most critical problems facing the internet of things and business today.

Chapter 14 – Yesterday, tomorrow and today

Here we look to the past to better predict the future and its impact. Some of the greatest glimpses into the future have been in the world of science fiction. Through this exploration we uncover some of the fundamental hopes and promises AI aims to achieve and deliver.

Chapter 15 – Next-Gen creativity: Improving the human experience

The question is: What does humanity do if AI lives up to its full potential and helps solves many of the world's major problems? The power of human creativity combined with AI will be fully unleashed for the good of business and the world.

Chapter 16 – The AI-infused future: Transforming the world

In the end, business and consumer power will drive and determine the course and success of AI. It's important to understand that AI is a tool, and it will be leveraged for good to unite the art of human creativity with the logic of science to create magical experiences to propel business and societal innovation for years to come. The opportunities for innovation with AI are endless, and it is our objective that you'll understand this more when you've completed reading this book.

PART 1

The AI foundation

CHAPTER 1

Changing landscape

Customer behaviours and expectation

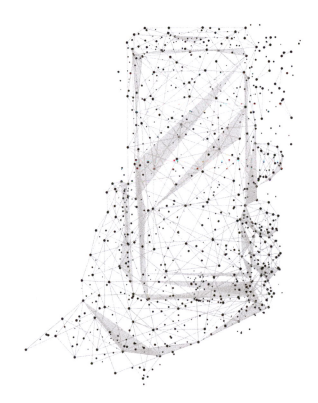

CHRIS Hey, Aimé. Welcome to the real world.

AIMÉ Hello, Chris. How are you today?

CHRIS I'm great, thanks. These are exciting times. However, it's a bit ironic that this appears to be a book about artificial intelligence when, in fact, it's not about this new emerging technology, but rather emerging cultural practices.

Service to humanity

AIMÉ That's right – the more things change, the more they stay the same. Ultimately, AI is about being of service to humanity. So, what we mean by that is, how can AI technology provide services, products and experiences that enrich people's lives? The goal with AI is not simply to build smarter machines, but rather to build smarter organizations, smarter societies and ultimately a smarter world.

But, you know, it's hard or even impossible to predict where AI and similar technologies such as internet of things (IoT), mobility and robotics will wind up in a decade or two. Just look back 20 years, and you can see that no one could have predicted the ubiquity of mobile devices and smartphones. Not even the science fiction stories from the last century envisioned this explosion of the internet into our lives.

Technology has changed our daily lives

CHRIS To that point, if we examine how our daily habits have changed because of technology, just look at how dramatically mobile phones have impacted everyone over the past few years. I remember flip phones that could only make calls, and now, in seemingly a blink of an eye, you have a powerful

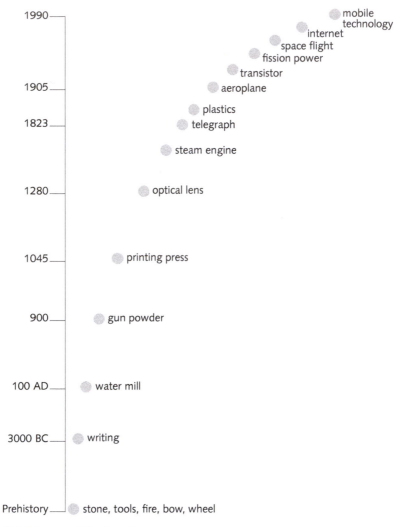

1990	mobile technology
	internet
	space flight
	fission power
	transistor
1905	aeroplane
	plastics
1823	telegraph
	steam engine
1280	optical lens
1045	printing press
900	gun powder
100 AD	water mill
3000 BC	writing
Prehistory	stone, tools, fire, bow, wheel

A history of technology

Awesome Science. www.tech-stress.com/1-2-history

computer, a high-definition screen and an internet connection in the palm of your hand.

Just the other day, I was walking around the supermarket and it was unmistakable how many people were so immersed in their mobile devices. They used their phones to compare prices with other stores, talked openly to their family members about what they needed, and scheduled Uber to pick them up after their shopping experience.

With those insights in mind, Adobe Labs has leveraged a technology called Adobe Sensei. Adobe Sensei, Adobe's AI and machine learning framework, is uniquely focused on

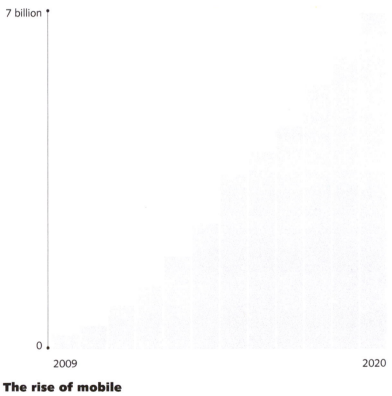

7 billion

0

2009   2020

The rise of mobile
Ericsson and Tune Forecasts

solving digital experience challenges – and, for example, can interpret live foot traffic in stores. The idea is to determine the habits and information about shoppers, such as products they typically purchase, demographic information and how much they spend. 'Imagine walking into a grocery store, toward the produce aisle, but then getting a ping on your phone that the cookies you bought last week are on sale. You add them to your cart, put your phone away and keep shopping.'[1]

AIMÉ Yeah, it's unquestionable that mobile electronic devices are playing an increasingly pervasive role in our daily activities. In 2018, American adults are expected to spend almost three and a half hours a day on non-voice mobile media, and 57 per cent of mobile users immediately check their smartphone as soon as they wake up.[2]

CHRIS It seems that people are always looking at their phones, and the statistics reinforce those observations. Just look at how people use mobile phones in their daily lives. Information services and social connections are pervasive, and it's common for individuals to wrap their vacations around using their smartphones to document every moment of their experience, posting a stream of photos and videos to their Instagram, Pinterest and Facebook accounts.

And, even more interesting, is how mobile is transforming the workplace. Looking back to the supermarket example, take Trader Joe's. They use mobile devices called line busters to speed up checkout at their more crowded stores. Additionally, the Apple store was one of the first to allow customers to pay directly from their iPhone, so they rarely see a checkout, or stand in line.[3]

AIMÉ People are online everywhere and all the time. Smart watches, smartphones and even wearable devices are connecting individuals to the internet 24 hours a day. There's even research into smart threads, which, when woven into clothing, produce the ability to change colours and patterns on demand.[4]

Because of this popularity, mobile sales continue to rise; 264 million Americans use their mobile phones 12 billion times a day. According to Deloitte, 'This year, smartphone penetration reached 82 per cent overall with ages 18–24 having the highest penetration at a staggering 93 per cent.'[5]

Mobile technology is dramatically improving the ability of business to increase their bottom line while enhancing service and reliability for both employees and customers. For instance, so-called smart factories depend on wireless technology to create a connected floor, effectively enabling them to be synchronized and optimized to fit changing conditions. According to Deloitte Insights, 'The ability to adjust to and learn from data in real time can make the smart factory more responsive, proactive, and predictive, and enables the organization to avoid operational downtime and other productivity challenges.'[6]

Democratization of information and accessibility

CHRIS Another perspective on the impact that technology has had on society is from a generational perspective. Consider that 18-year-olds (born in the year 2000 or later) were born into a world with mobile devices, social media, YouTube stars, tablets and, now, wearable devices. This is their reality and basic to their view of the world.

These digital natives see things differently because it's so effortless for them to communicate with anyone or anything at any time. It's normal for them to purchase a pizza online and have it delivered in just an hour, or even buy a car from their mobile or tablet. Their expectations have had a halo effect across not only generations but also across businesses.[7]

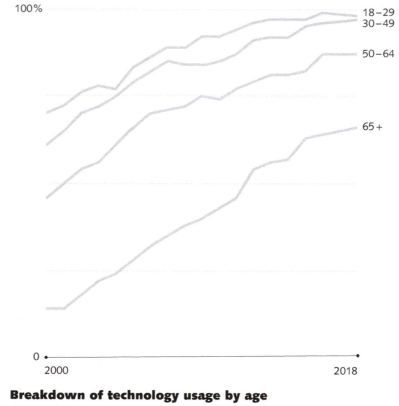

100%

18–29
30–49

50–64

65+

0

2000   2018

Breakdown of technology usage by age
PEW Research Center. Surveys conducted 2000–2018. Data for each year based on a pooled analysis of all surveys conducted during that year

AIMÉ Ultimately, this fulfils the initial promise of the internet, which was the democratization of information and accessibility to everyone. Just look at how Africa leapfrogged laptop and desktop technologies and is now becoming known as the mobile and connected continent. In fact, drones are being used in concert with advanced mobile technology to efficiently transport products across areas without developed transportation and communications infrastructure.

A company called Zipline delivers much needed, urgent medication by drone to rural areas in Africa and South America.

Business Insider reported, 'In Africa, use of drones is receiving more acceptance and [they] are increasingly being deployed for many activities. Countries like Cameroon, Morocco, Malawi, South Africa, Rwanda and Kenya allow the use of drones in tourism, health services and ecommerce industries.'[8]

The ubiquitous nature of the internet combined with mobile has given rise to the empowered customer. However, people are not just customers – they are humans. Businesses and brands must be of service to their audiences or they will find themselves obsolete and losing market share. Just look at the revolution caused by Uber and Airbnb to see how quickly companies that focus on fulfilling an unmet need and serve their customers will overtake more traditional businesses that focus on products and not experiences.[9]

Constant connections

CHRIS In the end, that translates to businesses being connected with their audiences wherever and whenever they are. This applies to a physical or digital setting across devices.

To take it a step further, media habits have drastically changed. It goes without saying that it's no longer solely about television commercials; the days of television shows designed around advertising that were created by a small number of rival networks are long gone. In the 21st century, it's about having personal, contextual and relevant conversations with actual human beings. In the very near future, virtual and augmented reality will change the relationship between businesses and consumers even more.

AIMÉ It's exciting that augmented reality (AR) is going to have an impact on retail, because we are now seeing that AR is embedded into many operating systems. Today you can walk into a physical store, hold up your smartphone and see how a shirt will look on you. Or, you go into your local grocery store, aim your smartphone at a food item and get a list of complementary food items for a recipe.

Another example is IoT, in which smart devices are becoming predictive and suggestive. A smart device can detect if you're tired by the tone of your voice and suggest you make a cup of coffee or suggest that it's time to take a nap.

In the internet of medical things (IoMT), a smart toilet can automatically take samples and monitor health. These tests can give the doctor a day-by-day understanding of how well a person's body is performing and enable serious medical conditions to be diagnosed well before they become dangerous.[10]

CHRIS Because of all this technology, it's never been more difficult to get people's attention, given the proliferation of ways to reach them throughout their environment. These include the rising use of mobile technology, the ability to access information across multiple screens and platforms, and new technologies like AR, wearable devices and voice.

Just look at Amazon's Audible platform. You can listen to an audiobook on your Amazon Fire TV, continue listening on your smartphone while in the subway, and finish the book from your Kindle sitting under a tree at the park. The Amazon ecosystem remembers your position within each audiobook, regardless of platform. It even works on non-Amazon devices using an app.

Uses of technology

AIMÉ That's precisely it. Attention is scarce, but when technology can save time and add convenience and speed, that's the true value for people and businesses. Take, for instance, outdoor advertising placed on skyscrapers and buildings in large cities such as Los Angeles and New York. These are becoming smart, in that the messages and images are not only programmed remotely, but even change from minute to minute based on visual or auditory cues in the environment.

If that's not complex enough, consider that work and life have become merged and intersect more than ever before. The so-called gig economy, which is growing in popularity, means that people can work for multiple employers anywhere in the world. They can do their jobs from home, the beach, the park or their office, as is convenient.

Digital artists now use applications such as Adobe products on their phone or tablet to create two- and three-dimensional (3D) graphics and even animations from anywhere and everywhere. They may never even need to step inside their office, since few applications require an onsite presence. In fact, as 3D printers mature, it will even be possible to create physical products from any distance.

CHRIS Going back to mobility, look at the transformation with online learning. Curriculums can be customized and personalized to fit an individual's exact needs, schedules and budgets, and the learning can be done from anywhere and at any time using mobile technology.

Companies such as Udemy offer short, concise and highly targeted courses with bite-sized content suitable for learning at convenient times including breaks, lunch and in between projects. This disruptive technology has the promise of completely changing the way education works into a newer, leaner model.

Collaboration

AIMÉ That brings us to the discussion about collaboration, where teams can work or play together at widely dispersed locations. Consider modern multiplayer games (known as massively multiplayer online games, or MMOG), where tens of thousands of people interact with each other and automated characters in real time.

Examples of virtual worlds are Roadblocks, Minecraft and Fortenight, and specifically Second Life, which allow individuals to live virtual lives within an artificial world. Money earned in that world can even be transferred to a real-life bank account, in effect creating opportunities to make a living as an avatar.

CHRIS Isn't it fascinating that not only the physical work and life worlds are merging, but the virtual world is also intersecting with both realities? I talked to a person who funded and built a café in Second Life, hired virtual waiters (people playing avatars), and now he makes a good living from his virtual business.

Disruptive technologies such as this are one of the reasons why *Inc.* magazine notes that half of the S&P 500 companies will be replaced in the next decade. Companies must transition to the new reality of digitization, which includes learning how to market more effectively.[11]

Marketing has become a dialogue

AIMÉ Yes, online marketing is no longer a monologue – it's becoming a dialogue. The buying process has changed to reflect the customer journey through multi-channel, multi-platform marketing. This has created a tremendous challenge because the buying process and customer behaviours have become so complex. Marketing and business communication must evolve to reflect these new realties.

Look at how internet advertising is evolving from simple banner ads to complex interactive social platforms that engage with people and target their specific needs and wants. For instance, take Facebook. It's no longer just a social platform – it is becoming a media outlet and central to the online life of many people all over the planet. Messages can be highly and precisely targeted with lookalike modelling and similar techniques.

CHRIS Case in point, just look at one example of a complex buying process. A person searches using social media, researches at review sites, compares styles across different websites or apps and then goes into the store to examine the product. Finally, the consumer goes back online and buys the desired product, which is delivered by drone to their front door.

The customer journey is essentially discover, try, buy, use and renew. And that is what makes measurability and attribution so challenging without the correct software. How can you directly link the effectiveness of an ad through such a complex buying environment?

AIMÉ The answer is leveraging widely dispersed and de-siloed databases and using predictive analytics to get a more holistic view and insights into marketplace dynamics and opportunity. This is the challenge for big data, and we will discuss this in more detail later. It's important to note that the data must exist and be accessible for AI to be successful.

CHRIS That's right, Aimé, there are a lot of leading-edge things happening with all these new technologies but it's really about putting people first. What do customers want and how can we go to them to help them fulfil their needs?

The true mission of artificial intelligence

AIMÉ The vital fact to remember is, none of these technologies we discussed are intended to replace human beings. Instead, humans and artificial intelligence will work together to create a brave new world, which we'll discuss later. This will be a world where people are freed to use their natural creative abilities and their amplified intelligence without concern for the drudgery of mundane, repetitive and, quite frankly, boring tasks. This is the true mission of artificial intelligence.

CHAPTER 2

The digital transformation

From messaging to experiences

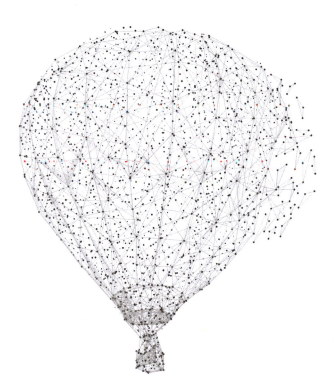

CHRIS We've established the cultural shift of the connected customer and digital disruption. Now we will talk about the need to create experiences.

AIMÉ As we talk, remember that I'm not human. Experiences are a bit of an abstract thought for me. I know the definition from the dictionary, but I don't really understand the application. In other words, I haven't experienced experiences.

CHRIS Ha. Great point. Thanks for the reminder.

86	1
%	%
of consumers who are willing to pay more to receive a better customer experience	of customers who feel their expectations are being met consistently

Brian Solis, *X: The Experience When Business Meets Design* (Wiley 2015)
CEI survey at www.oracle.com/us/products/applications/
cust-exp-impact-report-epss-1560493.pdf

Engaging experiences

One definition of architecting experience is by Brian Solis. He defines experience as the sum of all interactions of customer engagements with a brand or company. Brian talks about how the customer and business interact at every touch-point and every 'moment of truth' throughout the customer lifecycle. I'd like to add that this could be applied to other interactions, such as an employee's engagement with their employer, a patient with their doctor, a business to another business and others as well.[1]

AIMÉ That makes sense, but let's talk about practical applications so I can better understand how to apply the concept.

CHRIS Let's start with one of the true pioneers in customer experience, Amazon. A good place to begin is by looking at their logo. It's a smiling face, which indicates their focus on not only delivering products but also great experiences. People like smiles, and Amazon tells them, with their logo, they can expect to be happy with the service and products they receive.

AIMÉ Good point – the goal of delivering great experiences must permeate across an entire organization.

CHRIS Yes, that's just one of those touch points and it reinforces the message that customers will be happy with the whole experience from beginning to end. In others, they're saying you, the customer, will be enamoured with everything they do for you. That assumes they follow through with the implied promise of their logo.

AIMÉ They ensure the whole experience from the website, to ordering, to delivering on time, to handling complaints is optimized and frictionless for their customers. Their brick and mortar stores are designed to reinforce that ethos as well.

CHRIS But it doesn't stop there; Amazon's philosophy of providing the best possible service permeates their entire operation from their fulfilment centres to their delivery services to their website. Amazon design their warehouses to run at peak efficiency by clever and intelligent use of robots, logistics and even the placement of products to make it an optimized fulfilment experience.

And remember, now you can even order products directly by voice through Alexa.

AIMÉ Oh yes, I know Alexa, and I'm conversant with other voice assistants as well. In addition to smart speakers with assistants like Alexa Echo, there's Google Home and Apple Homepod.

With voice, there are huge opportunities for brands and companies to make things easy for the customer in meaningful ways. You could be brushing your teeth in the morning and ask Alexa about the temperature and traffic at the current time. It's all about delivering information, services and products tailored specifically for the customer.

That also applies in the business setting. Using their voices, physicians are now able to ask for the side effects of medications, truck drivers can plan their routes and managers can book meetings. The applications are endless, and the future is exciting.

CHRIS Don't forget virtual assistants such as Microsoft Cortana, Google Assistant and Siri. These are embedded and accessible on your phone, tablets and computers. In the future, you could even find these assistants helping you at the checkout in your local market and pumping fuel at a gas station. There is even an initiative called Product Box with the US Postal Service that is voice activated to make it easy to mail and track packages.

You can use a Domino's Pizza app on your smartphone to order pizza, which works as a virtual ordering assistant. Starbucks has its version, known as My Starbucks Barista, that allows people to order directly from their phone just like they were ordering from a real person in a store.[2]

There is a new, web-connected refrigerator by LG Electronics that lets people order their groceries (it integrates with Amazon Alexa) and even keeps track of expiration dates.[3]

These are just a few examples of how voice is enabling great customer experiences.

AIMÉ There are many things companies are doing to improve the experience at different touch points. Businesses need customers to survive, expand and compete, and customers are won over to a brand by a great experience. More importantly, a good experience means customers will come back again.[4]

Bloomberg Businessweek conducted a survey, and they found that 'delivering a great customer experience' has become an imperative for businesses. Eighty per cent of the businesses they polled put customer service as one of their top strategic objectives.[5]

Friction points

CHRIS Let's talk more about personalization and customization based on customers' preferences and previous habits and actions.

AIMÉ Businesses need to identify their customers' friction points, which are places along the customer journey that are not easy for them to accomplish, cause frustration or even result in abandonment of a purchase. Those are the moments of opportunity to enhance the customer experience.

CHRIS Netflix is a great example of successfully identifying and smoothing over friction points for their customers' benefit. Based on user history and past viewing habits, they predict and suggest shows and movies that may interest the viewer.[6]

Many banks require a detailed set of security questions to be answered to grant access to online, automated services. To make it easier on their customer, you can now enable voice authentication as a more secure and faster way to be positively identified.[7] Some banks recognize your phone number as another way to identify you without asking personal questions.

AIMÉ Speaking of banks, to prevent fraud with credit cards, a profile is maintained for each customer and card, recording their normal usage habits. This includes information such as their typing speed, navigation habits and even the pressure of their fingers as they press keys. If attempts are made to charge outside a standard deviation gleaned from their history, the fraud department is notified to call the owner of the card to validate the charges. This is an example of the benefits of understanding and knowing your customer habits and routines. On top of that, this works directly for the benefit of both customer and merchant credit card companies.[8]

CHRIS In healthcare, one of the friction points is the requirement to make a trip to the doctor's office and potentially experiencing extended wait times in hospital waiting rooms. To solve this dilemma, new telemedicine applications enable patients to use their smartphones to schedule appointments and then meet with doctors or other medical specialists remotely using text, voice or even video. Hospitals, doctors and insurance companies benefit from these trends by reducing visits to the emergency department and doctor's office for non-emergencies. Patients receive excellent care from a medical specialist or physician without the driving to a doctor's office and waiting in a germ-filled waiting room.[9]

AIMÉ Just look at what AppleKit is doing. You gather all your healthcare data into the app, then your smartphone makes suggestions based on your specific activities and medical needs.

It can remind you to take your medicine, stand up, breathe to lower your heart rate or remind you to do your exercise routines. That's a great use of personalization to improve customers' quality of life.[10]

Creating unique and interesting experiences

CHRIS Here's a brilliant future application of personalization on a grander scale. Consider a so-called smart city that knows about the schedule of sporting events. When an event occurs, the businesses could automatically be notified so they stock up on supplies, remain open later, hire temporary staff or run specials. Smart streets could monitor both vehicular and pedestrian traffic to automatically change routes, notify businesses or engage emergency services in the event of accidents. All of this could be done without human intervention.[11] In other words, an entire city could be personalized based on the habits and routines of its citizens.

AIMÉ That's an impressive example of innovation. Let's talk more about how personalization helps businesses with customer loyalty.

CHRIS Well, one thing to keep in mind is it's not just about one experience or touch point, it's about the whole customer journey. One moment of frustration from a poorly designed interaction can ruin the whole impression of the brand, causing the customer to look for other alternatives.

Let's look at the experience of purchasing a new car. There are phenomenal apps where you can design, build and customize your own car, based on the model and make of the brand. To take it even further, you can take a 'virtual spin', which is a simulation of a test drive. Let's assume you, our hypothetical customer, are delighted with the whole experience at this point.

Now, you use the app to pre-approve your credit, and within minutes you are pre-qualified for more than enough money to make the purchase. It even suggests a local dealer and handily offers to generate a map and make an appointment for you. You receive an estimate of the value of your existing car for trade-in and the app sends a text the day before reminding you of your appointment.

So far, so good. You are happy because you've designed your car to meet your needs, you have the credit, you know the value of your trade-in and the appointment is set up for you.

The big day of your appointment arrives, and you get to the dealer five minutes early. You quickly realize no salesperson has been assigned to you, which is a little frustrating, but you understand that sometimes things don't go perfectly. You may think the salesperson was sick or couldn't make it for some other reason.

So, you wait, and you wait some more. After 15 minutes, no one has even greeted you, so you ask the manager what is happening. He investigates the matter and tells you the appointment had never been forwarded them. To make matters worse, the car you so painstakingly designed is not only not in stock, but the extras you want won't work on that model. Now you are upset, which the manager understands and offers to personally help you through the problem. Unfortunately for her, it's too late, and you leave to look for a car another day.

As you can see, the experience began perfectly, but the glitches in a complex buying cycle derailed a high-ticket sale. The car dealer lost the business, the salesperson didn't receive a commission, and you didn't get the car you wanted.

This is just one hypothetical example of the need for carefully coordinated customer experiences. The complexity was introduced in this scenario because several different companies and apps were involved in the process and they didn't interface well together. The problem was caused by the failure to send an email or message to the dealer when the appointment was made. That simple error cost thousands of dollars and lost a customer for life.

To make matters worse, you were upset, and quite probably got on social media and posted an emotionally charged rant, left a negative review on Yelp and Google, and went on Facebook and told all 1,000 of your friends to avoid that dealership, potentially losing many more sales over the coming months and even years. This illustrates how one bad interaction can quickly snowball into a public relations challenge.

Of course, mistakes do happen occasionally. The answer is to ensure those friction points are also handled by the design of the overall system.

Suppose you want to order something online from Amazon. You jump on their website, which loads almost instantly, do a search, and within a couple of minutes find the product, read the reviews which are mostly positive, and make your order. Amazon offers same-day shipping in the cart, and since you want the product today you take them up on it. Even better, the service is free because you are an Amazon Prime member.

Unfortunately, the product didn't arrive when they promised, so you make a call to their customer service department. You talk to a real person, and within a few minutes they connect you directly to the shipping supervisor in your local area. She quickly identifies your package and determines it was delivered to the wrong address. She directs the driver, who is also on the line, to recover the package if possible and deliver it to you, even though it's late in the evening. An hour later your purchase is hand-delivered by a very apologetic driver. Within 30 minutes you get on social media to enthusiastically tell all your friends about the great service, effectively making you an advocate for the brand, despite the mistake that was made in delivery. The entire experience has been handled quickly, efficiently and, most important of all, to a successful resolution.

That's an example of building a tolerance for errors into a complex experience. Errors can always happen, and they are major sources of friction for customers and everyone else involved. If your system doesn't account for them, then you'll lose sales and your brand will suffer regardless of how great your products and services are.

As we just saw, it's no longer just about the unique selling proposition or price. Now, the focus is moving towards differentiation by creating unique and interesting experiences for customers and employees. Companies that thrive in today's marketplace have realized they are in the experience business.

Employee loyalty

AIMÉ True. The need for experiences is twofold. Businesses should create great experiences not only for their customers but for employees as well.

CHRIS For employees, a great experience not only increases innovation but also increases employee loyalty and retention.

A successful way to create employee loyalty is to build a sense of community and shared purpose, so the employees feel they have common goals with the organization. They understand they contribute to the success of the whole and reap the benefits of their efforts.

Because of this, individual employees don't feel like isolated cogs in a wheel without any real concept of how their efforts relate to what everyone else is doing. They know their jobs count and their voice is heard.

It goes beyond superficial perks. People are fundamentally hardwired[12] to connect with each other. When they have a sense of community, they have a better overall work experience, which increases their motivation and productivity.

A great example is Knowbe4, a company based in Clearwater, Florida. They gather the employees together in daily status meetings to quickly discuss important events, the goals of the day, how the company is doing and so forth. These are informal, and the team members sit in a circle on bean-bag chairs.

All team members share in the financial success of the company with a bonus plan in addition to their salary. If the company does well, so do all the employees.

Rituals of this nature help create a sense of purpose and community, and ultimately an ongoing great workplace experience. At the end of the day, employees will produce more and with higher quality as a result.

AIMÉ I'm interested in discussing how this translates to the customer experience.

CHRIS Motivated employees who feel they are part of the vision of a company provide better service, make fewer errors on the production line and have greater empathy for their customers.

Since the employees understand their purpose in the organization, and know the impact of their actions, they become more focused on delivering a better experience to their customers.

We tend to think of customers as those who purchase our products and service. However, it is important to understand there are internal customers as well. The internal IT department oversees repairing computer resources such as tablets, desktops and mobile phones. Their customers are the end users inside the company, and their role is to give a great experience to the employees of their company.

AIMÉ The interconnection of the overall experience architecture goes deep. It is clear that ecosystems are symbiotic in nature in that each individual part is dependent on how well every other part performs. Organizations are just another type of ecosystem.

In an experience culture, everything must work together like the finely tuned gears in a Swiss watch.

CHRIS This reinforces the need for businesses to put themselves in the shoes of the employee and customer. As we just discussed, experience design is very complex, and the true value of big data comes into play to unlock insights into how to personalize a great experience.

Building a great experience is not possible without the supporting data strategy and infrastructure. If you don't know your customers (and employees) then you can't give them a truly great experience.

The only way to understand your customer is to gather, maintain and analyse the information about their needs, habits and choices. If businesses have the foundation consisting of the data, they can take advantage of predictive analytics to understand their customers' experiential needs.

AIMÉ Well, if designing good experiences is complicated, our next discussion about data and analytics is even more so.

The experience culture

CHRIS Creating and maintaining an experience culture relies on information. You have to understand the behaviours, desires, and actions of your employees and customers in order to deliver exceptional experiences. That implies vast amounts of data must be collected, stored, sorted, categorized and understood rapidly and efficiently.

AIMÉ Without the data, it's impossible to provide optimum experiences.

CHRIS That's true, and it introduces a whole set of challenges. However, out of those challenges come phenomenal opportunities.

CHAPTER 3

Infinite data

Driving better outcomes

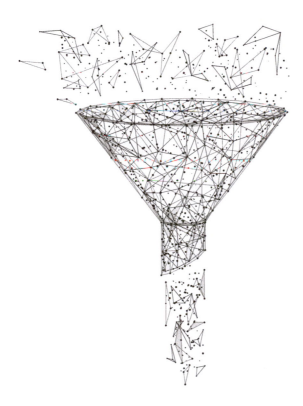

CHRIS Now, we're going to talk about data, which is the fuel of AI. Let's begin by defining data and where it comes from.

AIMÉ That's a big subject, and there's a lot to talk about, so let's get started. Have you had your coffee yet? Because we may be here a while.

What is data?

CHRIS Yep, let's get into it. Aimé, what's the exact definition of data?

AIMÉ According to the dictionary, data is 'individual facts, statistics, or items of information'.
A fact, such as your current location, is a data point, which means a single piece of data (one piece of data is also sometimes

2025

463

44

2016

Global data created each day (billion GB/day)
www.microfocus.com

referred to as a datum). Your phone number, bank account number and any other information about you are also data. A collection of several pieces of information is also referred to as data.

Your car's computer is collecting data all the time. The health of your engine is constantly monitored and recorded. Records of engine temperature, current mileage and even tyre pressure are maintained. The internal global positioning system (GPS), which is part of your navigation system, keeps a record of everywhere you have travelled. All this forms a picture of the health of your car and of your driving habits.

CHRIS Marketers are interested in data about their customers, which includes where people live, their demographics, their behaviours and preferences while they are online, and their search and purchasing patterns.

Electronic health records (EHRs) are now resulting in digitizing paper records into one source that houses all your health information. These older documents are combined with records from doctor visits, test results, allergies, medications and family histories. The information from all your doctors and specialists will be stored in one place that can accessed by your physicians, medical laboratories, medical imaging facilities, pharmacies, school clinics, you and anyone you authorize. These contain data from every source involved in your medical care. With complete and centralized patient information, your doctors and other medical providers can make better-informed decisions more quickly and safely.[1,2]

AIMÉ Imagine the amount of data generated by Amazon about the package you ordered today. They obviously know what you ordered and where it's going, but they also assign a barcode, so they can identify the package as it's transported to your location by a shipping company such as UPS, USPS, FedEx or Amazon's own delivery service. At any point, you can jump into their app and find out where your package was last scanned by the shipper. That's a lot of data for a single package!

But Amazon's service for a single package goes even further than that; the company is introducing Amazon Key, available for Amazon Prime members, that allows drivers to enter your home to leave your package inside where it is safe from thieves (parcel theft has become a major problem). When you order this service, you receive a webcam and a special lock that Amazon can remotely unlock to let the driver gain entrance. Amazon keep the videos to prove drivers' honesty. This gives Amazon even more information about you.[3]

The complexity of data

CHRIS Therein lies the power of data. Gathering all that information is the conundrum as it is labour intensive, complex and requires massive resources in the form of communications, infrastructure such as disc storage, and protection against hackers and unauthorized access.

AIMÉ Think about a company such as Amazon or eBay and their data. Let's follow and go into detail on a seemingly simple transaction from beginning to end.

To begin, each individual product unit is identified by a barcode, and all the information about it is stored in Amazon's database, including its dimensions, location in the warehouse, condition and everything else you can imagine.

When a customer orders that product, it must be retrieved from wherever it was stored in the warehouse and boxed up with any other products ordered by the customer at the same time. Amazon tracks not only every shipment, but every single product inside those boxes.

Now the box must be assigned to the appropriate delivery service, which could be the US Postal Service, UPS, FedEx, or Amazon's own service. A barcode is assigned to the box, which is sent to or picked up by the delivery company, who then forwards a record of shipment to the merchant. This is stored in the merchant's database; the package is delivered and the customer receives a text message and an email as confirmation.

Now, think about the number of touch-points of that process. The warehouse, shipping company, merchant (and possibly more than one of them), email, text messaging and Amazon's own computers and database. It's an amazingly complex operation, simplified so much that you are barely aware of what goes on behind the scenes for you to receive your package a day after you order it. And that's a simplification of the whole process, which is actually much more complex.

The point is that all the information, or data, about the transaction, is captured and stored on many servers (a specialized type of computer used by businesses) by many companies, and that information is subject to change in real time. All of it must be captured, organized and indexed, all the while maintaining a high level of performance.

Storing the data

CHRIS Then there is the question of where to store all this data.

AIMÉ Let's start with the concept of the cloud, which is actually very simple. In traditional computing, services are performed locally, meaning on individual computers onsite at the business. In cloud computing, those services are hosted on the internet, and may be next door, a hundred miles away or even on another continent. In fact, the business using the cloud service often doesn't know where the resources are located.

In many cases all information is stored in the cloud. For Amazon, they use AWS, which stands for Amazon Web Services. Google has a similar offering called Google Cloud Platform, and Microsoft calls theirs Microsoft Azure. There are other cloud hosting services as well.

Many companies create their own cloud services for internal use only; these are known as private clouds. It's becoming more common for businesses to use a hybrid model mixing external cloud services with internal, private cloud resources.

CHRIS As a side note, the accessibility of the cloud and the low cost has sparked the rise of SaaS, which means software as a service. Usually, these are applications which run in the cloud. Adobe Creative, Document and Experience Cloud and Microsoft 365 are good examples of this kind of service for businesses and consumers. In fact, we could write another book about the positive impacts of moving to the cloud, but that's beyond the scope of this discussion.

AIMÉ You can see how data storage can become very complex. A business's data can be stored locally in their own computer centre as well as on other computers across the country in the cloud. Additionally, they can access information from other vendors, customers and suppliers, as Amazon does with the postal carriers when they ship and track packages.

CHRIS We'll be talking more about the infrastructure needed to support all this data and computing later. For now, suffice to say that management of this vast array of data can be daunting, but the advantages for artificial intelligence are enormous.

AIMÉ Having all this information is fantastic, but it's not very useful if it can't be used.

CHRIS Yes, of course. After being gathered and stored, the data must be prepared to enable reporting, tracking, gathering of insights and so on in a structured way with good performance.

AIMÉ A case in point is that one of the biggest challenges with the internet of things (IoT) is connecting disparate devices with often proprietary data structures, communications media and interfaces.

CHRIS Aimé, now we're getting even more complex. Think of devices designed in different parts of the world, using different programming languages and with a different way for them to communicate.

Leveraging the data

AIMÉ What's exciting is the ability to leverage all this data to identify broad populations, use cases and trends using pattern recognition. Consider smart coffee makers designed to transmit a consumer's coffee drinking habits to the manufacturer. That information can be compared with the consumer's social media feeds to see if they are discussing the brand, and that can be correlated with other information to see if any trends can be determined. Some questions include: do those who brew more coffee make certain kinds of purchases, entertain more often or watch more television? Of course, some of this information would need to come from other IoT devices such as smart televisions and smart refrigerators.[4]

CHRIS Ultimately all this data is used for increased insights, profits and decision making. Part of the challenge is breaking down the silos and organizing the data.

Information is streamed from different sources. A merchandising company might store data in three departments – shipping, receiving and customer support. Each of these is a different silo of information. To get the most value, it's important to be able to see the broader picture by referencing data from all three silos.

This becomes even more complex when you consider there are also different types of data. For a customer, you need to store their phone number, which is one simple type of data, and their sales history, which is a more complex set of data.

Essentially there are two types of data sets. Structured data is organized in an easily understandable format. Examples include name, age, gender and date. Unstructured data comes from multiple sources and in different formats. YouTube videos, tweets, Facebook posts and comments are all examples of unstructured data.

According to OneUpWeb:

> Unstructured data is basically everything else – if it can't be easily classified, it's unstructured. User-generated content and user activity are a huge portion of unstructured data. This includes videos posted to YouTube (over 100 hours are uploaded each minute) and comments posted in social media accounts (510,000 comments were posted every minute in 2012 in Facebook alone). Unstructured data also includes information generated passively, such as GPS-location data generated by cellphones.[5]

Data strategy

AIMÉ I can see how that's important, but ultimately this all ladders up to a data strategy for better innovations, decisions and improvements.

CHRIS Like any strategy, it must be agreed upon within an organization and, if appropriate, across one or more others to be useful. As an example, information sent from a retail organization to its vendors and warehouses uses a standard called electric data interchange (EDI).[6] This allows information such as products, orders and so forth to be transmitted electronically. Obviously, the warehouse software must recognize the format of the EDI records to be able to use them.

Without agreed-upon standards, data becomes much less useful even for simple tasks and is useless for the higher functions such as artificial intelligence.

AIMÉ Businesses must practise both offensive and defensive data strategies. A defensive strategy is needed to meet regulatory requirements, reduce expenses, mitigate risks and fulfil other business objectives. On the other hand, an offensive strategy is intended to improve revenue, create new products and services, generate return on investment (ROI) and in general expand the business in some way.[7]

CHRIS Once the data strategy has been defined and agreed upon, that can create a significant competitive advantage. Look at PayPal's fraud detection. Their algorithms determine if a purchase is outside a standard deviation from normal. If so, the fraud department is notified and the customer might need to verify their identity, indicate they made the charge or the account might even be locked until the issue is cleared up. This gives the customer piece of mind because they know they are protected, and PayPal's brand is reinforced.

PayPal gained a competitive advantage by using a data strategy that backed up a fraud policy to put the customer first and protect their accounts and money. For this and other reasons, PayPal is one of the top payment processers in the world.

AIMÉ Because PayPal uses machine learning to continuously improve their fraud detection, even new types of malicious activities are quickly discovered and prevented. Their policy of incremental product improvements increases their revenue stream and helps them maintain their position in the marketplace.

The problem is always how to acquire and prepare the data, which must be captured, formatted, filtered, structured, indexed and manipulated before it's useful. Raw information does not do anyone any good because it cannot be used effectively. According to the *Harvard Business Review*, '80% of the work involved is acquiring and preparing data'.[8]

CHRIS Additionally, data must be stored and processed, which has time and cost implications. Infrastructure such as disc farms and computing power is required in large volume to get the work done. We'll talk more about infrastructure later; it's a big piece of the puzzle for AI, and it's not one-size-fits-all.

Cisco estimates that the IoT will generate more than 500 zettabytes (a zettabyte is 1 trillion gigabytes) of internet traffic per year by 2019.[9] All that information needs to be stored somewhere, then categorized and indexed to be useful.

AIMÉ Part of the reason Walmart is so successful has to do with their logistics and supply chain. That company grossed $476 billion in the 2014 fiscal year, manages more than 4,100 stores and operates a huge supply chain to distribute products from vendors and warehouses to their stores. Because their supply chain is optimized, they save time, manage inventory more cost effectively and improve product forecasting. Walmart invests in emerging technologies to improve the efficiency of their supply system. They use data they gather from all points in the distribution system to help with demand planning, forecasting, inventory management and other areas.[10]

CHRIS That's a great example of using data as a strategy to improve the business. Walmart, like many retailers, was affected by the 2008 recession. They used both an offensive and defensive strategy to remove 'thousands of marginal SKUs off its shelves to reduce store clutter, focus on faster-growing product categories and improve supply chain efficiencies.'[11]

There are countless other examples because every business has a data strategy, regardless of whether it's formally defined. If businesses don't state or think through their strategy, one gets defined for them. A small business might not think about data, but they use information regardless to solve business problems. Even a business consisting of a single store verifies credit cards, orders inventory and so forth. Thus, all businesses, regardless of size, leverage data to fulfil their needs.

AIMÉ There are a multitude of considerations, from technical requirements to implementation to daily usage, all the way to how all this fits into the information technology strategy for the business.

CHRIS Remember, a business must begin by defining its strategy, then all parts of the organization must align and work together to fulfil it. Data should be driven by the business strategy, not the other way around; businesses struggle when they allow data and infrastructure to drive their strategy.

It's common for businesses to restrict their growth based on their infrastructure and data models. This behaviour makes their reaction opportunities sluggish and tends to limit their expansion.

AIMÉ Back to our earlier discussion, businesses prosper when they put customers and employees first. As noted in the *Harvard Business Review*, 'Google, Amazon and others have prospered not by giving customers information but by giving them shortcuts to decisions and actions.'[12]

CHRIS Quite often, a company's infrastructure is not easily scalable, and it doesn't keep pace with the business strategy. This can hold back expansion and allow the competition to gain a bigger foothold than they otherwise would. Suppose you have a retail business with a strategy of global expansion of 50 stores within a year. If the business hasn't invested in infrastructure and a data model that is scalable at that rate, then that goal will not be realized.

AIMÉ Isn't that the truth? It seems that infrastructure is very important.

CHRIS Infrastructure is vital. That was a gripping discussion around data. It's nice to see how it's this mix of art and science, the creativity of pulling out insights with the logic of being systematic. One prediction is that some of the most innovative ideas are going to come out of traditionally left-brain-based (logical) disciplines.

AIMÉ I think we should now spend some time talking about solutions that are scalable and cost effective.

CHAPTER 4

Infrastructure

The need for a foundation

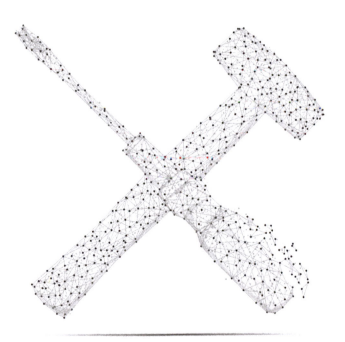

AIMÉ Chris, how many software engineers does it take to change a light bulb?

CHRIS I don't know, Aimé.

AIMÉ None. That's a hardware problem.

CHRIS Funny. Speaking of hardware, AI requires an infrastructure. By this, I mean decisions need to be made as to where the applications, both AI and non-AI, will reside. Will they be hosted locally in a computer room owned by the business or in the cloud, or a mixture of the two? That basic decision will drive what infrastructure needs to be built.

Also, infrastructure includes communications, the network, computer rooms, discs, virtualized machines and anything else needed to support the applications. You could think of infrastructure as the workbench on which the applications reside.

Challenges of infrastructure

AIMÉ One of the biggest challenges of infrastructure is that most companies do not have the luxury of building from scratch. In other words, they must deal with legacy systems vital to operating the business while expanding existing and building new systems. This can complicate the process of expanding and modifying the infrastructure.

Obviously, companies must continue to operate as they expand and add on to existing infrastructure, build new facilities or take greater advantage of offsite (cloud) infrastructure. Sometimes this is relatively simple, as when plugging in a new disc cabinet. In other cases, it can mean building an entirely new computer room and switching over to it when complete. You can also have a hybrid approach, where the old infrastructure continues to operate even after the new equipment is running.

This latter case often occurs when legacy applications cannot be moved to newer equipment.

CHRIS Let's look at an existing grocery retail company that has painstakingly built merchandising, logistics, customer relationship management (CRM), accounting and other systems along with the supporting hardware and applications.

AIMÉ As with many retailers, the merchandising system is highly customized and uses an obsolete database application and hardware that is no longer supported. The application was designed years before, and not only is the company that did the work no longer in existence, but the senior designer, the only person who understood everything completely, passed away.

One grocery chain depended on customized applications that had been operating successfully for over a decade. Those applications used an obsolete database platform called Unidata and ran on the OpenVMS operating system on VAX hardware. Unfortunately, the grocery chain outgrew the application and was forced to replace it with newer technology.

They decided to migrate the existing merchandising data over to an Oracle-based system running on newer, more advanced hardware with an entirely new set of applications. Other systems, such as payroll, were migrated to software as a service (SaaS) offerings, and their accounting system was converted to SAP, the software corporation that makes enterprise software to manage business operations and customer relations, and was running on top of Microsoft SQL.

In each case, hardware had to be purchased and deployed, networks installed, operating systems and databases set up and the existing data converted to entirely new applications. The older, legacy systems had to remain in place until the new ones could take over.

The whole process took place over several years and required an immense amount of planning and coordination.

Legacy systems

CHRIS An advantage of startups is they don't need to worry about legacy systems. Those companies have the advantage of beginning with a clean slate.

AIMÉ For the retailer we were just talking about, they had decisions to make. Could they continue operating using the old applications, database and hardware? If so, do they hire and train technicians to support the system? Or do they build a new application and the infrastructure and move the data over to it when it's ready? There are advantages and risks to every approach, and they must be thoroughly understood and seamless to prevent risk to the business.

Once the decision was made to move off the old hardware, database and applications, new questions needed to be answered. Should applications be maintained in house or outsourced to outside vendors? Was SaaS appropriate in some cases? What hardware, network and databases should be selected? What were the staffing requirements for each option? What about disaster recovery and business continuity?

CHRIS I remember being told about a retailer who hired a firm to create a new application to replace their merchandising system. Unfortunately, after spending several million dollars on development and much faster hardware, when they went live the new application performed poorly. This was puzzling because the new hardware was on the order of one hundred times faster, yet the ordering application went from two minutes per order to almost an hour to process the same order. When they investigated, they found a bug that hadn't been caught by the testing suite on the quality assurance system. Once they fixed that, the performance improved but was still worse than the older application. After spending over a million dollars, the database and applications were brought up to reasonable performance levels.

AIMÉ What we're saying is, the infrastructure was designed correctly to support the merchandising system, but the application and database had inefficiencies and programming bugs.

CHRIS Precisely! The problem here was the infrastructure was not designed with dedicated testing systems that replicated the production environment. What that means is the application could not be tested in real-life scenarios, which resulted in performance problems and errors when the application was run in live situations.

Infrastructure architecture

AIMÉ It's important to understand the whole picture. Why don't we take a step back, and talk about infrastructure architecture? What does an IT infrastructure look like?

CHRIS Essentially, infrastructure can be thought of as several layers. First is your network and second is your hardware, such as servers and disc drives (or the cloud-based equivalents). For the sake of this discussion, operating systems and virtualization should be done at this time.

It's becoming more common for businesses to use resources based in the cloud. This has many advantages, including lower cost, high performance, high availability and disaster recovery. However, using the cloud requires a larger investment in your network and communications, since the work is being done offsite. Some businesses use a hybrid model, keeping some applications and data in-house and running others in the cloud.

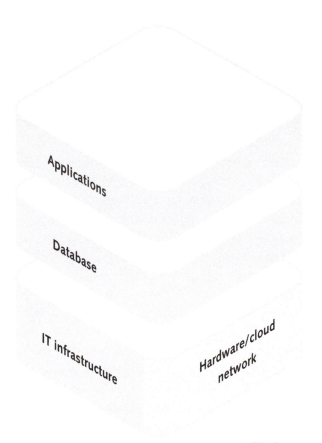

Layers of infrastructure

A third option is SaaS. This essentially can entail outsourcing an application, or service, to a third party. The concept works best on applications that don't require a high degree of customization, such as payroll or accounting. In some cases, SaaS is run onsite, but usually it's done remotely; you can think of it as an application in the cloud.

Many companies use a combination of in-house, cloud and SaaS-based applications.

The size of your network and communications will strongly impact your decisions. If your connection to the outside world is a T3 at 44.736 Mbps you'll probably find it's too slow to take advantage of SaaS and the cloud. On the other hand, an OC-48, at 2.488 Gbps, will give you much more freedom to choose. Of course, all this depends on many factors – for smaller companies, a T3 may more than suffice.[1]

Once you've decided where to host your data and applications, you can define your data model, because you need to know the speed of your communications, network and computing resources before you design your data. For SaaS offerings, the data model has already been defined by the vendor, but you may need to build imports and exports to get information from your other systems to and from the SaaS-based applications.

When you have a data model, you can define your databases, including which database application you use. Oracle and SQL are both excellent choices, each with their own strengths and weaknesses. Your choice may be constrained by the skill set of your IT department. It's not uncommon for a shop to use both the SQL and Oracle databases (as well as other choices) due to constraints forced on them by applications and vendors.

After your databases have been created, you can implement your applications. These include business-critical programs such as merchandising, accounting, logistics, payroll and so forth, as well as custom or specific applications for your users and company.

At the same time, you can start defining your artificial intelligence apps to run on top of your database and use the information maintained by your applications.

Remember, you must also consider staffing and management requirements for this entire infrastructure. Most businesses use in-house IT staff to run their computers, network and applications, while others outsource some or all of it. One common approach is to use the so-called 'gig-economy' to hire out projects on a piecemeal basis – this is essentially hiring freelancers when and where needed. Naturally, a combination of some or all the above methods may be used.

Designing your infrastructure

AIMÉ Technically speaking, infrastructure typically means your building, network and the servers and other hardware. Applications and databases run on top of this infrastructure.

CHRIS I completely agree, and we're simplifying it for the purposes of this discussions.

And other things must be considered as you are designing your infrastructure. It's vital to ensure everything is designed to be scalable, meaning you can add additional resources as the business expands without redesigning or re-implementing your architecture.

AIMÉ Yes, and high availability and disaster recovery are also concerns. The best practice is to implement those at the hardware or virtualization layer to make things easy. In the early days of computing, disaster recovery was implemented either via backup and restore, or programmatically in each individual application or database. That's very complex and prone to error. With modern technology, hardware or virtual machines can do the work for disaster recovery independent of any applications, which makes it easier and more robust.

CHRIS Let's go over each of those in a little more detail.

Disaster recovery

AIMÉ Business continuity is the plan for the business to continue operations after an emergency or disaster. It's concerned with keeping the business operating in the event of a disaster.

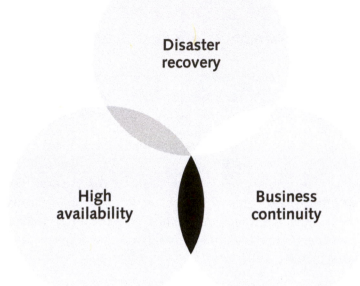

Disaster
recovery

High
availability

Business
continuity

Where will people work? Do they have the equipment they need to do their jobs? How will they get there? What about vital records?

CHRIS Yes, that last one is important. Many companies keep voluminous amounts of information on paper, even today. These could be as simple as Rolodex card catalogues that the salespeople use daily. If a building cannot be entered, those Rolodex cards cannot be used.

AIMÉ Accounting departments often have boxes and file drawers full of invoices and other records. If a fire or other disaster occurs, those records are destroyed or unavailable. This is one of the concerns addressed by business continuity.

CHRIS I know. Disaster recovery is typically the IT-specific implementation for the computing resources. Businesses need both because business continuity is not the responsibility of IT, as it is concerned with the larger picture.

AIMÉ High availability means redundancies are built into the design of the computer resources, so if something fails the systems continue working. Mirrored disc drives are a good example of this.

As a business becomes more reliant on cloud and SaaS services hosted offsite, the network and communications become critical. To prevent service outages, multiple links are often configured. A computer room can be designed with more than one OC3, for instance, and those could even be from different communications carriers. (OC3 technology is a type of bandwidth transmission. It stands for Optical Carrier 3 because it carries data on the third level of a synchronous optical network.[2])

CHRIS With all these computers, it's important to take special care to ensure power is redundant and backed up with uninterruptible power supply (UPS) and generators. Of course, that's assuming the hardware is local to the business.

AIMÉ That's one of the huge attractions to cloud and SaaS services – most of these concerns become the responsibility of vendors. For instance, Amazon AWS is redundant, built to survive disasters, and even managed by someone else. It's important to verify that the vendor follows high standards for their services.

CHRIS I know we got a bit technical here, but these considerations are important to the livelihood of businesses. They must be considered for companies to prosper under even the worst conditions. Non-technical people need to understand the importance of these issues.

Changes in technology

AIMÉ One of the guiding principles of technology is change becomes exponentially more difficult as you proceed through the process. Errors are easiest to correct in the preliminary design, more difficult once coding starts, even more difficult once the databases have been populated and extremely difficult once it's all in production. That's the advantage of the agile and scrum techniques – these tend to keep the teams aligned and catch errors more quickly than the traditional waterfall approach. We discuss these techniques in detail later.

CHRIS If you are off by just one degree, after a foot you're only going to miss by .2 inches. But if you travelled to the moon, you'd be off by 4,169 miles. It's far easier to correct at the beginning, when it's just .2 inches.[3]

AIMÉ That's true. One last point – avoid the leading edge (sometimes called bleeding edge) on infrastructure if possible. Unless there is a fantastic benefit to going with brand new technology or services, you'll generally have a better and more stable infrastructure by sticking with tested solutions that have withstood the test of time. New operating systems, even new versions, tend to have bugs and performance issues that are worked out over time. Unless you have an overriding reason to upgrade right away, it's safest to wait a short time to let the problems shake out.

CHRIS That's great advice.

AIMÉ We'll discuss this in more detail later, but always be aware of security and privacy as you design your infrastructure. Security works best when it is designed in from the beginning and it is a major focus of everyone involved in the process.

CHRIS Now that we've discussed infrastructure and data, we have the foundation for AI.

PART 2

The AI activation

CHAPTER 5

Artificial intelligence

The what and why of the AI revolution

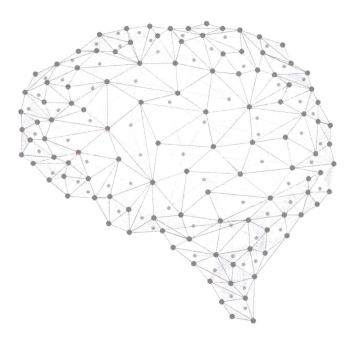

The Fourth Industrial Revolution

CHRIS Many have said AI is going to have an impact on humanity at the same level as the invention of electricity.

AIMÉ Yes. Some are calling it the Fourth Industrial Revolution, and they claim it will cause the most dramatic change in human society in history. To put that in perspective, McKinsey recently noted AI is advancing 10 times faster and at 300 times the scale of the Industrial Revolution.[1]

CHRIS Consider what AI can accomplish. Autonomous driving could change the trucking industry, in effect virtually eliminating accidents and improving delivery times. Smart cities could reduce energy usage and pollution, and improve the quality of life of inhabitants. There will even be smart factories, which will make products that are identical without flaws, smart mining, which will eliminate deaths due to cave-ins and toxic fumes, and smart farms, which could increase food productivity by several times while reducing water and fertilizer usage.[2,3,4,5,6]

Consider dengue fever, one of the most virulent viruses in the world. Microsoft is working on a robotic mosquito trap that can distinguish one insect species from another. Small lasers are used to individually target the tiny insects. Since dengue is mosquito-borne, the robot could be used to combat the virus by killing the mosquitos.[7]

The idea of AI being used to fight dengue fever without using pesticides – that's a game-changing application demonstrating how the technology will change human society.

AIMÉ The possibilities for the betterment of humanity are endless. To that point, Marvin Minsky in his book *The Emotion Machine* called AI a 'suitcase word' in that it contains 'many smaller concepts that can be unpacked and analysed'. This essentially means that the phrase 'artificial intelligence' has such broad meaning and application that there is not just one way to define it.[8,9]

1st Industrial Revolution

2nd Industrial Revolution

3rd Industrial Revolution

4th Industrial Revolution

1760–1840	1860–1900s	1770s–2015	2016–?
Machine-aided production	**Industrialization Technological revolutuion**	**Internet era**	**Machine to machine Smart automation**
textiles	factory electrification	computers	driverless cars
steam power	mass production	SAP	smart robotics
machine tools	assembly lines	B2C	internet of things
coal power	telegraph	B2B	3D printing
	TV and radio	the cloud	global sourcing
	conveyor belts		true automation

The Fourth Industrial Revolution

www.raymondjames.com/forefront/industrials/text/welcome-to-the-fourth-industrial-revolution

Today, AI is defined as 'the study and design of intelligent agents', which are systems able to perceive their environment and act based on what is happening. The subject of AI overlaps with computer science, data mining, facial recognition, robotics and others such as the study of the human mind.[10]

That brings up an interesting point. To fully understand artificial intelligence, we should talk about human intelligence.

Human intelligence

CHRIS A lot of people think intelligence is measured by a thing or a test, but actually human intelligence can be categorized into nine types, according to *Multiple intelligences: New horizons in theory.*[11]

The nine types of intelligence are intrapersonal, spatial, naturalist, musical, logical-mathematical, existential, interpersonal, bodily-kinæsthetic, and linguistic. Of course, everyone has all these components to a greater or lesser degree. Some are strong musically while being weaker spatially, while others are strong in the existential area but are introverted and thus have less in the interpersonal area.

Consider Donald Knuth, who is well known for his mathematical abilities and for writing *The Art of Computer Programming*, but not so much for his musical talents. Contrast that with Bach, who was strong in music but weak in logical-mathematical. Or take someone like Leonardo da Vinci, who was an equal balance of a scientist and an artist. It is commonly believed he said people should 'study the science of art and the art of science'.[12]

However, people are holistic in nature – they do not normally fit into just one category. Herein lies the complexity of artificial intelligence, the purpose of which is to try to re-engineer the human mind to a certain extent.

As we'll discuss later, there are different opinions about the ethical use of AI, both pragmatically and philosophically. The

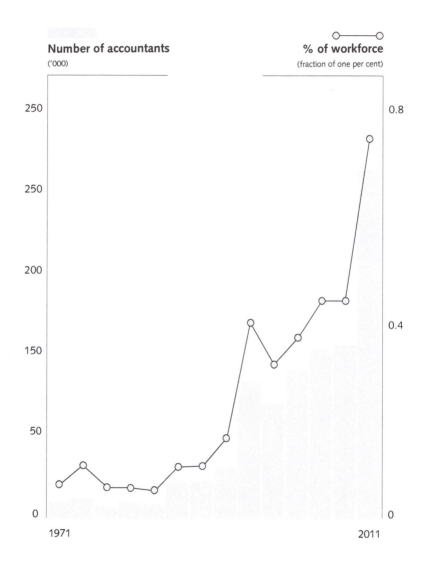

Number of accountants
('000)

% of workforce
(fraction of one per cent)

How technology has boosted jobs in knowledge-intensive sectors

England and Wales Censuses 1971–2011

possibilities of AI to change human society and interaction are endless, and as with any new, radical technology there will be side effects. One concern is the effect on jobs, another is how AI will affect human behaviour and interaction, and a third concern is security and protection from those who would use AI for questionable purposes.[13]

Regarding the effect on jobs, Daniel Lacalle put it best:

> Evidence shows us that if technology really destroyed jobs, there would be no work today for anyone. The technological revolution we have seen in the past 30 years has been unparalleled and exponential, and there are more jobs, better salaries. The best example is the German state of Bavaria, one of the parts of the world with a higher degree of technification and robotization, and with 2.6 per cent unemployment. An all-time low. The same can be said about South Korea, and the world in general.[14]

In 2015, researchers in Singapore performed a trial of a smartphone app that tried to use AI to influence decisions of actual people. The idea was to build a personalized model of how much individuals were willing to accept delays in public transportation. The information gathered could be used to help reduce congestion and crowding to keep people who are travelling happier with the services.[15]

AIMÉ Those are great points about the types of intelligence, the effect on jobs, and how AI can influence people and society. With that said, let's chat about how AI evolved to where it is today.

Cycles of AI

CHRIS In the summer of 1956 researchers at the University of Dartmouth came together to create a machine that acted and thought like a human, with the goal of creating an artificially intelligent being. This vision for AI was quite advanced,

77

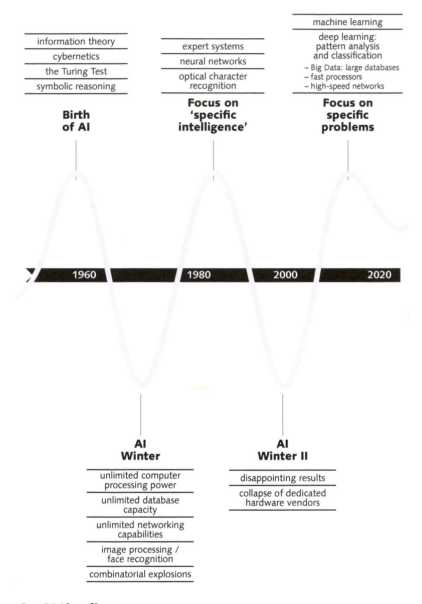

information theory
cybernetics
the Turing Test
symbolic reasoning

**Birth
of AI**

expert systems
neural networks
optical character
recognition

**Focus on
'specific
intelligence'**

machine learning
deep learning:
pattern analysis
and classification
– Big Data: large databases
– fast processors
– high-speed networks

**Focus on
specific
problems**

1960   1980   2000   2020

**AI
Winter**

unlimited computer
processing power

unlimited database
capacity

unlimited networking
capabilities

image processing /
face recognition

combinatorial explosions

**AI
Winter II**

disappointing results

collapse of dedicated
hardware vendors

An AI timeline
www.harmon.ie

78

considering the best technology of the time was a mainframe using punching cards.[16]

What followed was a series of boom and bust cycles, six or seven times, when people got very excited because of a break-through or two, but then became disillusioned when the results didn't live up to the expectations. These cycles are known as 'AI winters', which is a term taken from nuclear winters, which were the concern during the 1950s. It was believed that a nuclear attack would create conditions that would make life difficult or impossible – a nuclear winter. The analogy was that funding dried up for a few years after a boom in AI, mak-ing it difficult or impossible to develop it more.

In 1966, the first AI winter happened when researchers realized the difficulty of language translation. At the height of the Cold War an attempt was made to leverage AI technol-ogy to interpret 60 lines of Russian text and translate it into English. The initial results came out looking pretty good, but when they translated the text back into Russian they realized the experiment was a failure. This exposed the complexities within human language. Funding for experimentation dried up for several years and led to the first AI winter.[17]

Jump to 1970, when the second AI winter, known as the Microworld, began. The boom began with the idea of con-straining the number of variables, so the experiment is bet-ter controlled. For example, let's have a computer arm take block A and move it over to block B. Those micro-interactions worked well, but the researchers realized the idea was not scalable. This led to the second AI winter.[18]

In 1980 the third AI winter began, due to experiments with expert systems. The idea was to remove all the variables to create something that's scalable – design from the top down rather than the bottom up, by going to individual experts within their fields and codifying their knowledge into a series and sets of rules. They interviewed each expert and then programmed their knowledge. Unfortunately, the effort of building an expert system was so time-consuming and costly that the initiative failed. This led to the collapse of the expert system, which began the third AI winter.[19]

However, in 2012 a breakthrough happened, because of the development of a subset of artificial intelligence called machine learning, more specifically known as deep learning. Neural networks work in a manner like the human brain, and the result is computers that can learn. Today, all the major technology companies including Apple, IBM, Amazon, Microsoft, Facebook and Adobe are leveraging and contributing to the acceleration happening within the AI landscape.[20]

AIMÉ Exciting times for AI, and not just because virtual assistants like me came into being.

AI successes

CHRIS Speaking of acceleration, just look at some of the major AI successes over the last 15 years. In 1997 IBM's computer Deep Blue beat Garry Kasparov in a chess tournament. Before that, it was commonly believed that a machine could never beat a chess grandmaster. And in 2005 a self-driving vehicle completed the DARPA self-driving challenge, which was a first for autonomous cars.[21,22]

AIMÉ In 2010 Tony Fadell created the first smart thermostat for use in a smart home. As you know, the internet of things is made up of smart devices such as intelligent thermostats, light bulbs, alarms and so forth. All that started in 2010 with Tony's success.[23]

CHRIS And just one year later, in 2011, IBM Watson beat Ken Jennings at Jeopardy. Quoting H G Wells via Homer Simpson, Jennings wrote, 'I for one welcome our new computer overlords.' In the same year, Siri was introduced for the iPhone 4S, revolutionizing speech recognition on a mobile platform.[24]

AIMÉ One of my favourite breakthroughs was in 2012, when Andrew Ng and Jeff Dean created and showcased technology that recognized images such as cats within videos. This was a huge step forward for image recognition.

That's an example of a visual breakthrough. For audio, Amazon Echo assistant was released to the world in 2015. This allowed consumers to take advantage of AI voice control to order products, turn on lights, get recipes and so on in the comfort of their homes. This is just the beginning of the voice interaction revolution.

In 2015 Google's deep mind team created AlphaGo to play the boardgame Go, defeated Fan Hui 5 to 0, and went on to beat world champion Ke Jie 60 to 0 in 2017. 'AlphaGo's ability to crack the game of Go means it is capable of sophisticated pattern recognition.'[25]

And in 2017 Libratus beat top human professional players at the game of no-limit Texas hold'em poker. This showed AI could learn the broader contextual understanding involving probability and reasoning.[26]

AI is gaining steam in business, industry and the consumer markets.

Types of AI

CHRIS That's true, especially when you consider that we're only at the beginning of the AI revolution. To break it down a bit, there are essentially three forms of AI: narrow, general and superintelligent.[27]

When we talk about modern AI, we're talking about narrow AI, which means artificial intelligence that's designed to perform specific tasks. Google Search is a great example of a discovery task, and it's become ubiquitous in its use throughout the population. AI chatbots are Q&A algorithms that can answer customer questions, and these AI applications can assist with customer service and help customer representatives with suggestions about what would be most valuable to the customer.

General AI, known as artificial general intelligence (AGI), is the notion that at some point AI will have human-equivalent intelligence. By that, I mean that it has a holistic understanding of its environment and can make conclusions on its own based on multi-sensory inputs without specific programming. AGI is achieved when AI intelligence is indistinguishable from human intelligence.

Superintelligence is a notion that is often represented in Hollywood movies, which anthropomorphize AI to an exponential increase of intelligence over humans. AI is represented as all-knowing as able to solve problems and questions well beyond human capability or even understanding.

In this conversation, we're discussing narrow AI and its practical application.

AIMÉ The label 'narrow AI' doesn't really do justice to what AI can do. Contrary to the implications of the term, the capabilities are vast. Narrow AI includes machine learning, deep learning, natural language processing, computer vision and machine reasoning.

CHRIS Let's define those phrases, with the caveat that they are somewhat loose terms in which disciplines and techniques overlap to a certain extent.

By machine learning, we mean the ability of an AI application to learn from the environment with and without programming. For instance, the time people spend on the road commuting to and from work has steadily increased; in 2014 this resulted in $160 billion in lost productivity. AI is helping to tackle these complexities so those lost hours on the road can be reduced. Now, traffic analytics coupled with AI is able to analyse and learn from commuter data to help manage and improve traffic and road infrastructure conditions.[28,29,30]

Deep learning uses neural networks, mimicking the biological function and structure of the human brain. One excellent application for neural networks is the recognition of handwriting. That's an extremely difficult task to program, but neural networks learn and then automatically infer the rules.[31,32]

A use case for AI is natural language processing (NLP), which uses machine learning and deep learning to analyse, understand and use human language in a useful way. Essentially, NLP can understand and generate spoken and written language and put the two together. In the legal world, NLP is used for document classification.[33]

An additional application for machine learning/deep learning is with utilizing a combination of computer vision and machine reasoning. For example, humans look at things and understand them instantly; 'we can each look at a book and understand what it is and what it does even if we have not all got the same nuanced understanding of what goes into its making and what happens around it'. Machine learning/deep learning can now enable computers to solve this challenge – with computer vision and machine reasoning, a cognitive system can have the ability to recognize and understand objects.[34]

The Massachusetts Institute of Technology (MIT) breaks narrow AI down by role instead of technology. One of these is the assistant, such as semi-autonomous cars that include a human driver for more involved driving situations. An example of this is Mobileye, which is an advanced driver assistance solution that helps drivers avoid accidents. This company was founded in Israel and the product is currently installed in many public buses, helping human bus drivers to avoid accidents.[35]

AIMÉ And then there are different types of machine learning. These include supervised learning, unsupervised learning, semi-supervised learning, active learning and transfer learning.

CHRIS To go even deeper, here are some categories of deep learning. These include unsupervised pre-trained networks, convolutional neural networks, recurrent neural networks and recursive neural networks.[36]

AIMÉ These techniques can be used to create some powerful things. However, one of the challenges with machine learning is that it still can't explain how it came up with a prediction or a solution. Because of this, AI is referred to as a black box.

CHRIS I know. No commercially available system currently can explain its thought processes.

AIMÉ However, machine learning and deep learning truly excel at sensing and predicting patterns. This makes these techniques useful for parsing out written and spoken data, faces from images and videos, and so forth.

CHRIS These techniques are scientifically fascinating, and they are propelling the digital transformation forward for consumers and businesses. AI is one of the fundamental drivers of the digital transformation occurring at warp speed across social, mobile, web and cloud, and even in the real world.

AIMÉ Isn't that the truth. And this isn't even hypothetical. AI is making a huge impact on business-to-business issues, including the areas of workflow, processes, supply chain, ecosystems, predictive intelligence, customer service chatbots, nurture, social media, SEO, landing page and content management.

CHRIS And on the business-to-customer side of things, AI is having an equally huge effect, not only in the end products, but also in their creation. AliveCor is a wearable IoT device that tracks electrical activity of the heart (electrocardiography – ECG or EKG) on demand and detects normal or irregular heart rhythms. Another take on medical EKG measurement is from a company called Happitech, which uses the sensors on your smartphone to measure your stress, fitness levels and so forth.[37,38]

AIMÉ In these cases, AI was used to create the product as well as within the finished product.

AI combined with other technologies

CHRIS The success of AI is amplified by and will evolve with other technologies.

The internet of things uses AI for many different functions. AI can be implemented to build bridges between different devices, as well as being embedded into each individual 'thing'. Consider a smart refrigerator that learns your family's eating and drinking routine so that it can order before products run out. VAIDU monitors the weather to remind you to take your coat and umbrella if rain is predicted.

For the industrial internet of things, entire smart factories can build automobiles or anything else without human intervention except for a few supervisory and technical personnel. This relieves humans from the drudgery of the assembly line and eliminates the need to expose people to hazardous industrial situations. Other applications include smart mining, smart warehouses, smart ships that are completely crewless, and so on.

The applications in the medical world by the internet of medical things are enormous, and Allied Market Research predicts the IoT healthcare market will reach $136.8 billion worldwide by 2021. Smart medical devices can monitor various parts of the body to enable doctors and patients to be better informed about their condition and improve health. AI can be used to discover patterns from the data reported by all these devices and give accurate feedback to guide healthcare decisions.[39,40]

The retail experience is being revolutionized by augmented reality (AR). The Ikea AR app allows people to view their catalogue products, over 2,000 of them, anywhere in a room. You just bring up the app on your smartphone, hold it up to an area of your house, and place the furniture anywhere in the room.[41,42]

AIMÉ Speaking of the medical world, there are some incredible things happening with pain management. Virtual reality is being used as a therapeutic tool to help people with their pain during painful procedures, as a soothing, calming technique prior to surgery and as an educational device. In 1996 virtual reality was first used to reduce the pain of burn patients at the Harborview Burn Center in Seattle, Washington.[43,44]

CHRIS We could get into a discussion about blockchain, and I'm sure it has many applications in AI, but that's probably a subject for another book. Essentially, blockchain is a distributed ledger useful for sharing information such as crypto currency, health records, legal contracts and so forth. It relates to AI because a blockchain is a way to store large amounts of data in a secure manner and, as we've been discussing, AI is based on data.

AIMÉ AI provides a great solution for renewable energy. One of the problems with renewable sources such as wind and solar is the unpredictability of weather patterns. Energy provider Xcel, based in Colorado, is using AI to attempt to solve this problem by mining data from the National Center for Atmospheric Research, giving it a higher level of accuracy and detail. This is just one example of AI's impact on renewable energy.[45]

CHRIS I'm excited by what's happening with biotechnology. AI is now being used for more than just helping identify diseases; it's helping pharmaceutical companies to identify molecules that are useful for therapy development. In this and other ways, AI is being used to help researchers in biotechnology.

AIMÉ I'm even more intrigued by the technology of medical 3D printing. You've heard that 3D printed organs can be printed from a patient's own cells? In a few years, this means that organ transplants may consist of 'printing' organs rather than harvesting them from human bodies. 3D printing can also be used to print airplane engine and motor vehicle parts and even to repair a damaged satellite. In the consumer market, 3D printing could print broken parts, eliminating the need for shipping or visits from technical personnel.[46,47]

CHRIS The European Space Agency is using 3D printing to print models of asteroids, then using those models to train satellites using AI on how to detect and avoid collisions.[48]

AIMÉ But, at some point, we will get close to the limits of the ability to process data with current computer technology. Quantum computing is a mind-blowing new way to process information, and in the words of D-Wave:

> A quantum computer taps directly into the fundamental fabric of reality – the strange and counterintuitive world of quantum mechanics – to speed computation. Rather than store information as 0s or 1s as conventional computers do, a quantum computer uses qubits – which can be 1 or 0 or both at the same time. This quantum superposition, along with the quantum effects of entanglement and quantum tunneling, enable quantum computers to consider and manipulate many combinations of bits simultaneously.[49]

The point is that faster computers are being developed continuously with more power, and that will enable AI to be that much more powerful and useful going forward.

CHRIS What is really thrilling is nanotechnology, because it looks like it could be a potential cure for cancer as well as many other diseases. Nanotechnology works with particles that are the size of molecules that enable scientists to directly target and repair or destroy invading or cancerous cells.[50]

There has been research into nanotechnology and AI that's enabling stochastic processes. A stochastic process is a process that has a random probability distribution that can be analysed statistically but not predicted precisely. This can, in theory, allow better understanding of the biological environment variables.[51]

AIMÉ You know, that's a fascinating notion. A random statistical algorithm could be used to create unexpected correlations that could assist creative thinking.

CHRIS Speaking of creativity, this is how AI is being used in innovative ways in coordination with these other technologies. People refer to AI as being as significant as electricity, and this is what they are referring to – how AI is going to power so many advances in technology and improve human life and society.

AIMÉ It's enlightening to see how AI is being used in these leading-edge technologies, but also how it can be applied to further creativity, empathy and emotions.[52]

CHRIS We've just chatted about the technical aspects of AI, but more important is how computers and people work together to make more intelligent decisions, provide better service and give optimal experiences. This goes back to one of the founding principles of AI, which has to do with intelligence amplification.

Next, let's talk about how AI can be used to improve and amplify business strategy. AI strategy essentially boils down to a set of tools to give businesses strategic advantages in their marketplace.

CHAPTER 6

The SUPER framework

A superhuman strategy

AIMÉ Now that we've laid the foundation of the technical aspects of AI, let's unveil the strategic model that will unleash extraordinary competitive advantages for you and your business.

CHRIS We're calling it the SUPER framework, and it will provide superhuman capabilities. SUPER is an acronym for speed, understanding, performance, experimentation and results. It's a powerful five-pronged model that harnesses AI as a catalyst for innovation.

The SUPER model provides five guiding principles that are necessary for successful AI implementation. These serve as the basis for an AI roadmap on which a strategy can be built. All five prongs – speed, understanding, performance, experimentation and results – must be addressed by your AI strategy for your project to succeed.

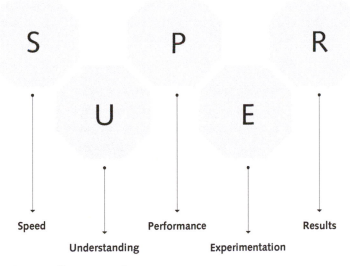

The SUPER framework

The SUPER framework explained

AIMÉ Yes, that's true. To be *successful,* an AI strategy must first be designed around speed. Consumers and businesses will not tolerate solutions that do not produce results quickly. Imagine an AI-driven telemedicine application that takes several days or hours to give a person an assessment about their illness. A mother with a sick child wouldn't tolerate that kind of response time.

CHRIS Of course she wouldn't. AI must also address *understanding.* AI-enabled solutions must produce a greater understanding of a problem or situation. Consider an AI product that serves as a home alarm system. You would expect that system to learn about the environment and visitors, and then make decisions based on that information. Such an alarm system could see over time that some people are never granted entry while others are always granted access to the building. Operating autonomously, the AI-enabled alarm could foreseeably grant or deny access based upon what it had learned, regardless of whether a person had a key or password.

AIMÉ Any AI-enabled product or solution must accomplish what it was designed to do – *performance* of its given task and goal. For instance, a so-called smart ship, which operates without any crew on board, must not only be able to navigate, but it must also be able to learn what to do during adverse weather conditions, understand how to handle a boarding by an unauthorized party such as pirates, and know what to do if it detects that a possible collision is about to occur.[1]

CHRIS Then there is the need for *experimentation,* which forks into two aspects: curiosity within the AI model itself and how AI can spark curiosity and inspiration. Curiosity and inspiration are often needed to solve complex problems where the solution is not obvious or readily understandable. This inspiration can drive the development of new use cases and applications, and is essential to the process of developing this technology. According to MIT, 'a computer algorithm equipped with a form of artificial curiosity can learn to solve tricky problems even when it isn't immediately clear what actions might help it reach this goal'.[2]

Additionally, products, even AI-driven ones, don't operate in a vacuum. There is always competition, which drives the need for improvements in the technology. Additionally, unexpected conditions and unplanned circumstances inevitably arise, and these may require experimentation, research and development to produce more advanced versions as time goes on.

AIMÉ Finally, AI strategies must have *results* that impact the business's bottom line. Whether AI is used for products or services that were recently commercially launched or are mature in the market, businesses expect results.

CHRIS Now let's discuss each aspect of the SUPER framework in a bit more detail, because there are nuances. For instance, in some cases, AI projects may emphasize one or more of the prongs over the others. All aspects must still be part of your AI project; however, your strategy may focus more on one or two depending on your requirements.

Speed

AIMÉ Let's start with speed, by which we mean increasing the velocity of work and reasoning, or getting to a starting point more quickly. For instance, if you want to improve customers' experience of getting through an airline check-in procedure more efficiently, you'd focus on optimizing their traffic flow. One airline company, Trans States Airlines (TSA), has been testing a new system that could accelerate the speed with which travellers pass through security at the airport. It uses AI to evaluate the facial expressions and posture of travellers to point out any that may pose a threat to security. Body scans are not shown to TSA screeners to ensure travellers' privacy is protected; TSA personnel will only be alerted about those who might pose a threat.[3]

Understanding

CHRIS AI can access vast amounts of data very quickly, revealing and interpreting that information to provide insights into marketing, customer behaviour, healthcare, automotive, driving habits and so on. Combined with IoT and similar technologies, the possibilities for comprehending the world around us are unlimited. Netflix uses predictive analytics to understand customer preferences and make predictions to provide optimal recommendations. The recommendation engine not only connects viewers to the content they want to see, but it improves over time. It learns about customer tastes and distinguishes between what people say they want to see and what they really like.[4]

Performance

AIMÉ When we talk about performance, we mean efficiency, which measures the effectiveness of the process. In this respect, we're concerned with how well the job, service or product is or has been performing.

AI strategies and their application must be measured and optimized on their performance and how well they are supporting the overall business strategy. In other words, those strategies must pay off, and that must be measured, quantified and reported to various stakeholders. Key performance indicators need to be defined before the AI initiative is begun, to measure business-level success.

CHRIS There's a startup in Copenhagen that's working on a camera system that uses deep learning AI to detect where the action is on the soccer field. The idea is to automatically zoom in on the action and follow the ball. This is significant because the majority of matches are not recorded because a lot of teams cannot afford to hire a camera crew to record all their games.[5] Ultimately, this technology greatly reduces the need for large camera crews because the cameras can now work on their own.

The startup used a deep learning framework and trained the neural networks to track the ball and players consistently and accurately. This AI product must be fast enough to track and record the soccer match. It must also learn and understand how to follow the action, especially the ball on the field, meaning it must build an understanding. The creation of the product is the result of innovation and curiosity, and as the product matures its tracking performance will improve.

This is an example of an AI product that supports a business strategy; popularizing soccer by recording more games, which in turn exposes it to a larger audience. All of which requires specific KPIs that measure business-level success.

AIMÉ That's a compelling use for artificial intelligence for performance purposes. The upside is enormous, because the sports industry in North America has been projected to reach $73.5 billion in revenue by 2019. This comes from gate revenues, media rights, sponsorships and merchandising. AI chatbots can automatically respond to fan inquiries, computer vision can guide cameras to take better still and video images, AI journalism helps media outlets with their sports coverage, and wearable IoT devices combined with AI will be used to gather data for training and performance optimization.[6]

Experimentation

CHRIS AI also ushers in a new era of experimentation, by allowing for faster interactive processes, meaning supporting minimum viable product (MVP) feedback loops; creating, testing and optimizing. Also, AI inspires new approaches to products and services that were unimaginable in the past.

Results

AIMÉ Finally, AI must produce results that support businesses, consumers and industries. PayPal, for instance, uses deep learning to detect deceptive merchants and pinpoint sales of illegal products. In addition, their models optimize operations by providing an understanding of why transactions fail. Both these solutions improve the ability of PayPal to deliver service to its customers by cutting down on fraud and improving reliability.[7]

Superhuman capabilities

CHRIS The SUPER framework will unquestionably provide superhuman capabilities. SUPER is based on the high-level premise that humans and machines working together are more powerful than individuals working by themselves. Whether you are creating software, solving problems or inventing new products, these principles are all designed and tested to enhance the role of humans rather than replace them.

In 2014 AI was used to amplify human performance in chess by 'marrying human intuition, creativity and empathy with a computer's brute-force ability to remember and calculate a staggering number of chess moves, countermoves and outcomes'. They called this new type of chess player, the combination of human and AI, a centaur.[8]

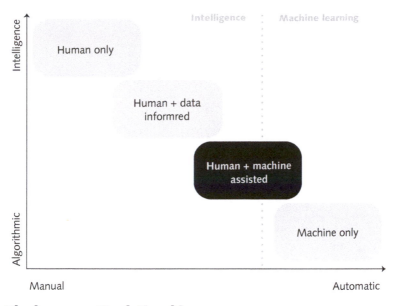

The human + AI relationship

This notion is known as the human/AI system. In this relationship of combined human and AI power, one best practice is to begin by defining the roles for people and the roles
for AI. People are best suited to perform some types of task,
while AI has the skills to best perform other roles. AI excels at
storing and remembering huge amounts of data and making
very complex calculations based on those data sets. People
are extraordinarily skilled at social interactions and complex
tasks, among other things.

Keep this in mind when trying to determine who should
do what; let humans do what they do best and AI do what it
does best. This combination results in the best approach to
problem solving. Thomas Malone refers to this concept as
collective intelligence,[9] which is the concept that intelligence
arises with groups of individuals – families, companies, coun-

tries and armies. When you put human intelligence together with computer intelligence you open up a whole new range of possibilities.[10]

AIMÉ To break that down further, AI can be looked at as an assistant, a peer or a manager.

An assistant, a peer or a manager

CHRIS Adobe Sensei is Adobe's AI machine learning framework that is used to dramatically improve the design and delivery of extraordinary digital experiences. Practically speaking, that means Sensei can be leveraged as a creative assistant within content creation and distribution functions.

Imagine you are creating an app and a creative graph would be mapping out every major decision within that creative process. At any point, you would be able to go back and see what the end output would look like if you had made different decisions.

Semi-autonomous cars are a great example of AI working as an assistant. Systems such as the Audi Traffic Jam Pilot and the BMW Traffic Jam Assistant help by taking over steering,

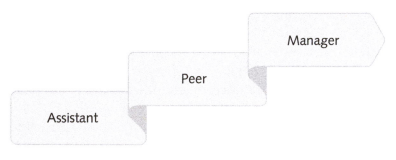

The role of AI
https://x.ai/blog/our-future-relationship-with-robots

braking and accelerating during heavy traffic. Because they are intended only to assist, they require you keep your hands on the wheel even when they are manoeuvring.[11]

IBM's Watson technology powers innovations such as Watson Virtual Agent to allow businesses to provide automated services to their customers and analyse those services to provide insights on customer engagement. This technology helps with understanding customer needs as they evolve over time.[12]

AIMÉ Another example of an AI assistant is the KLM Customer Service Rep Tool. This AI-powered deep learning application helps customer service agents deal with 'the overwhelming volume of messages coming at them via social media and other channels'.[13] The application, known as DesignGenius, pulls information from historical customer data, social media and a wide variety of other sources, and the results are used by applications such as Zendesk or Salesforce Service cloud.

To make Facebook more relevant for their users, the company collects posts by you, your friends, your groups and every page you've liked – on average between 1,500 and 10,000 posts. Proprietary algorithms, driven by a combination of AI and human reviewers, analyse this data and decide how information will be displayed on your newsfeed.[14]

CHRIS An example of AI operating as a peer is in Football Play Predictions. Two students at North Carolina State, William Burton and Michael Dickey, built a system to predict whether an NFL team would pass or run. In a 2014 game featuring the Cowboys versus the Jaguars, the model was right 91.6 per cent of the time.[15]

AIMÉ This is an intriguing way to use AI, and it can also be used as a manager. In 2015, commuters in America spent over 8 billion hours stuck in traffic. Stephan Smith, a robotics professor at Carnegie Mellon University, equipped traffic lights in Pittsburgh to use AI to react to traffic patterns as they changed. By doing this, travel time was reduced by 25 per cent.[16]

Airlines generated $168.2 billion in revenue in 2016, and traffic is projected to double in two decades. Because of this, airlines are looking into how AI can help them keep up with the demand and improve their service. AI is being used to help customers on the phone as AI assistants, to improve airline logistics and to use facial recognition to speed up identifying customers.[17]

CHRIS Another benefit of this symbiotic relationship is that humans and AI learn together and from each other, in addition to each improving over time.

Imagine an AI assistant for physicians that scanned thousands of records from cancer patients including their X-rays, MRIs, doctor's notes, electronic health records and even their exercise and eating habits. From analysing that data, the AI health system can advise physicians, who learn from this to provide better care for their patients. For instance, when doctors are presented with a rare disease they may miss the symptoms if they haven't encountered them before. These AI assistants could make the correlation and flag patients for additional tests or diagnosis.

AIMÉ That reminds me of the machine learning components used by Malwarebytes to detect new forms of malware that have never been seen before in the wild. Signatures won't catch new viruses and malicious applications because their pattern has not been recorded. Thus, AI must be used to analyse behaviours and point out the deviations from normal that might indicate an infection. These potential issues are then analysed by humans to determine if they are actual malware.[18]

CHRIS These are wonderful examples of how humans and AI can learn and improve from each other.

Supporting business strategy

AIMÉ Ultimately, AI strategy is intended to serve and support business strategy. To reference Michael Porter in his book *Competitive advantage: Creating and sustaining superior performance*,[19] there are essentially three universal business strategies. They are cost strategy, focus strategy and differentiation strategy.

CHRIS By cost we mean lowering prices to consumers to gain competitive advantage as an overall strategy. There are essentially two ways to accomplish this goal:

1 Reduce the cost to the consumer

2 Reduce manufacturing costs

Two gold standards to this approach are Walmart and Ikea. Walmart has branded itself with the tag line 'Save money. Live better' to reinforce low costs in the minds of consumers. Their strategy has been so successful that they are one of the world's largest retailers; in fact, if Walmart were a country, it would rank 28th in the world in gross domestic product, right behind Norway and ahead of Austria.[20] That shows the power of providing value at a low cost, so much so that Walmart has over 11,000 stores worldwide.

AIMÉ Tell me about it. Did you know that Walmart sells over a billion pounds of bananas per year?

CHRIS I didn't know that, but it doesn't surprise me. Ikea offers low costs to its customers by combining the economy of sale, giving them leverage to negotiate with vendors and integrating technology into their business processes. They offer a great selection of products (9,500 different items), update their product range yearly and are aggressively expanding internationally.[21]

AIMÉ Walmart is using AI, machine learning, the internet of things and big data to improve all aspects of their business, from logistics and supply chain management through manufacturing and customer service.[22] Ikea is using AI to create an augmented reality application and pursue other ways to improve customer service.[23]

CHRIS That's astounding. The second business strategy for business advantage is the differentiation strategy. Tesla and Harley-Davidson are great examples of how well this strategy works.

Elon Musk disrupted the automotive industry by introducing a mass marketable electric car. He saw the need and opportunity, and he designed not only a car but also an entirely new energy system, manufacturing plant and logistics chain.[24] Tesla had to create the infrastructure for all four tiers of manufacturing from tier one, which is the final manufacturer (in this case Tesla), through tier four, which is the supplier of raw materials.[25]

Harley-Davidson is one of two major motorcycle manufacturers to survive the Great Depression. Their brand is based on freedom of movement, and their slogan is 'All for freedom, freedom for all'. They created a product and a culture based around a lifestyle of freedom and independence, which differentiates them from other motorcycle brands.[26]

AIMÉ Businesses that concentrate on a particular, well-defined, narrow niche can create competitive market advantage. This is the 'focus' business strategy. Take Trader Joe's and Starbucks, both of whom have identified their customer base and deliver an experience that satisfies their needs.

Trader Joe's private label their products, which means customers cannot find them anywhere else. They also focus on creatively designing products and even decorating their stores. In fact, many stores hire a full-time artist to create signage, artwork and murals that are specific to the area where each store is based.

When you think of Starbucks, you think of quality coffee made exactly the way you want. This is core of their brand, and an example of how a business can have a narrow range of products yet still have broad appeal in the mass market. Starbucks takes it to the next level in terms of focusing on their customer needs by being able to infinitely customize their coffee. You could, in theory, order the concoction half caf/half decaf coffee, hold the foam with a teaspoon of skim milk and a dash of chocolate.

The main point with these examples is that AI is a tool that should be aligned with your company's strategic approach and support the overall business strategy.

We discussed how business strategy falls into three buckets, and how AI can be used to address or amplify each one. For instance, in terms of the focus strategy, AI can help identify consumer behaviours through predicative analysis. For the differentiation strategy, it can identify market gaps that can be exploited or expanded. For the cost strategy, it can leverage to create logistic and manufacturing efficiencies.

CHRIS Now that we've identified the three overarching business strategies, let's discuss how businesses can specifically unlock AI's potential using the SUPER framework.

CHAPTER 7

Speed

Facilitating work processes

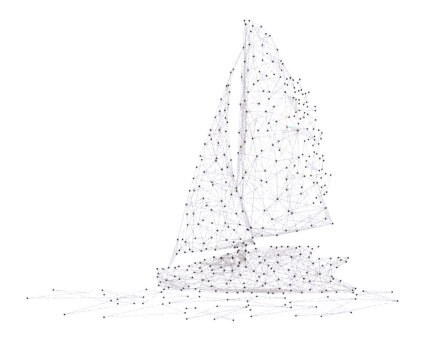

CHRIS Sometimes big results come from the smallest things. In the inaugural modern Olympic Games in Athens in 1896 one runner, Thomas Burke, crouched at the start in a four-point stance, which was new at the time. Because this gave Burke a slight advantage, he won the gold medal 12 seconds later. This shows that even the tiniest change makes a huge difference to the end result – much like the idea that, according to chaos theory, the flapping of a butterfly's wings in New Mexico can cause a hurricane in China.[1, 2]

Restrictions on growth

AIMÉ One of the restrictions on how quickly a business can grow is how fast they can create the products that they sell to other businesses, the government and consumers. If a company can only create 10,000 units of a product in a year, they can only sell 10,000 units in that year. On the other hand, if they can build a million units, they can sell a million units.

CHRIS That's very true. In 1913, Henry Ford revolutionized the automobile industry by creating the assembly line, which reduced the time needed to build a new car from 12 hours to 2 hours and 30 minutes. By June of 1924 one of his factories had built 10 million Model Ts.[3]

AIMÉ The Japanese auto makers built world-class production facilities in the United States and implemented practices such as just in time (JIT) delivery of parts to their factors and lean manufacturing. By improving manufacturing processes and making their supply chain more efficient, these automakers dominated the industry for decades.[4]

CHRIS Ironically, the quest for organizational speed can often paralyse or slow down an innovation product because it can overwhelm the organization, employees, consumers and individuals.

Sometimes, though, an emergency or critical situation can spur tremendously fast growth. An example is aircraft production in the United States during World War II. In 1939, fewer than 6,000 planes a year were being produced, and the entire aircraft industry was 41st in size when compared to all other industries. By the end of the war, the industry was the largest in the US, had produced 300,000 military aircraft and operated 81 production facilities across the nation.[5]

However, under normal conditions businesses and individuals may not be able to change direction that quickly or maintain an extremely high velocity. That's where the philosophy of Kaizen comes into play. Instead of quick, sudden, disorienting moves, it's usually better for change to be instituted incrementally, a little at a time. This gives people a chance to adjust and incorporate those changes into their normal routine.[6]

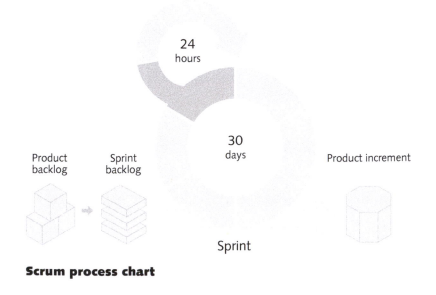

Scrum process chart

Agile and scrum are development methodologies that have been adopted by many organizations to iteratively develop solutions that are the result of collaboration between self-organizing cross-functional teams. The purpose is to deliver high-quality solutions that align with the goals of the company and the need of consumers in the least amount of time.[7] Agile describes a set of methods and practices emphasizing that developers and the business collaborate closely using self-organizing teams with a focus on delivering business value. Scrum provides a framework allowing people to address complex problems using collaborative teams.[8,9]

Organizational acceleration

AIMÉ Now organizational acceleration is more accessible and achievable because of advancements in technology, as illustrated by Moore's Law, which states that computer speed and processing power will double every two years. This is an area where AI can be of tremendous benefit by enabling people, processes and technology to unlock acceleration, speed and velocity.[10]

CHRIS A good example of this is Adobe Sensei, which is a framework of AI technologies that powers intelligent features across Adobe products to dramatically improve the design and delivery of digital experiences, using artificial intelligence and machine learning in a common framework.[11]

One major focus of Adobe Sensei is to address content velocity with shorter time to results. Content velocity is driven by the need and expectation of personalized experiences, and as a result marketers, brands and agencies are encountering the need for more content creation at a higher rate of speed. Adobe Sensei can help speed up content creation, distribution, measurement and optimization.

To illustrate, photo search speeds up the search for images in image collections because Adobe Sensei can autotag images for faster and more specific searchability. Using AI-driven image recognition technology, content creation is accelerated because the tedious task of tagging and searching for the exact right image is automated.

One area where AI provides considerable benefit is automating paperwork. Machine language and artificial intelligence can complete paperwork for support calls, which enables customer service people to focus on helping customers rather than filling out forms. This improves the customer experience, increases their loyalty, give you a good reputation and streamlines operations. Additionally, AI can analyse the calls themselves and find patterns that indicate problems and products or services that can be corrected.[12]

Carrying it a step further, AI chatbots can fully automate common customer service issues. By doing this, you can provide support 24 hours a day, seven days a week, provide rapid answers, eliminate training of personnel for common problems and increase your customer engagement. Additionally, chatbots tend to make fewer errors and provide proactive customer interactions.[13]

Manufacturing

AIMÉ Manufacturing is also a complex process and multiple variables make it prone to performance challenges, lack of efficiency and production errors. These issues limit the scalability of the manufacturing process and the amount and complexity of product that can be delivered.

Nintex Workflow Cloud is developing a particularly exciting application for manufacturing. Rather than focusing on creating robots or AI solutions for individual tasks, this company examines the entire workflow of the manufacturing process, looking for behavioural patterns, issues and bottlenecks. The AI then suggests changes and improvements, which can range from adding automatic escalations, to automating repair processes, to the procedures associated with bringing on new employees. This results in an optimized, faster manufacturing process.[14]

In 2016 robotics company FANUC partnered with technology company NVIDIA to use their AI chips to build factories of the future. Essentially, they are using AI, specifically deep learning, to allow industrial robots to train themselves. This cuts down on training time, speeds up the ability to change processes and improves the performance of the assembly line. The result is faster training for faster factories that change direction more quickly.[15]

Siemens is using AI, specifically neural networks, to optimize wind turbines so they can learn from wind patterns and autonomously adjust the rotors on the turbines according to the wind direction. This increases the amount of power generated by a wind farm because it operates more efficiently. This is an instance of using AI to quickly adapt to environmental conditions and thereby improve output.[16]

It's interesting to note that 'lights out' manufacturing operations and AI are different. In some types of artificial intelligence, machines learn how to perform better, and in effect teach themselves. In 'lights out' manufacturing, machines run with no human interaction without necessarily using AI. On the manufacturing floor, everything happens in real time and historical reporting has no value.[17]

Medical

CHRIS In the medical field, patients often learn they have a severe problem when they go to the hospital. By that time the condition has often become serious and irreversible damage has been done. Medical conditions such as heart failure are hard to predict. Jianying Hu, a programmer at IBM Research's Center for Computational Health, wondered if they could predict the problem in advance by identifying hidden signals buried within electronic health records (EHR). In a three-year, two-million-dollar research project, IBM mined the health records of more than 10,000 people, using an AI computational model.[18]

IBM's Watson for Genomics and Watson for Oncology are currently available to doctors and scientists, and a project called Medical Sieve is using AI to identify instances of breast cancer and cardiac disease. DeepMind was founded in London in 2010 to build AI technologies to help society. DeepMind Health is part of this initiative, and the goal is to help patients, nurses and doctors by supporting the National Health Service (NHS) and other healthcare systems. All of these, and other, initiatives are designed to speed up everything from getting customers in the door of a hospital, all the way through to advanced diagnosis.[19]

AIMÉ Those are great examples of AI being used to improve the speed of medical diagnosis and patient care. There is much work ahead, because AI in healthcare is relatively new, but the promise of the technology is profound.

Retail

CHRIS Another area where speed is important is getting people through checkout lines. It might seem mundane, but there's little worse than waiting in a long line at the theatre, a grocery store or a theme park. Solving this problem improves customer satisfaction, gives them a good reason to come back and helps prevent negative social media reviews.

Traditionally, stores that commonly experience long lines must ensure their point-of-sale system processes purchases quickly. The backend systems must be reliable and perform well, and employees need to be trained with a focus on getting customers through the lines quickly. Line busters, which are mobile units that can be used to check out customers from anywhere in the store, can also be used to speed things up even more.[20]

New technologies such as AI-powered body scanners will help speed up lines at the airport by automatically identifying questionable items on a person.[21] This will be used to accelerate getting through security at the airport.

Two new startups, New Zealand's IMAGR and Silicon Valley's Mashgin, are working to create enabled systems that add up what goes into a shopping cart as the customer shops. With this technology, combined with mobile payments, the checkout line could be avoided entirely.[22]

AIMÉ That brings to mind what AI can accomplish to improve the entire experience and speed of shopping. Customers want their shopping experiences to be highly customized to reflect their personal choices, and they want to get it done quickly. Customers would like to walk into a clothing store, for instance, and be presented with a variety of clothes and accessories matching their tastes as soon as they arrive.

Personal shopping assistants are being developed to make personalized experiences a reality. Retail management firm BRP did a survey in 2017 and found that 45 per cent of retailers intend to implement AI to improve customer experiences.[23,24]

The advantage to customers is that as they shop, they will be presented with exactly the items that they need and want, whether they realized it or not; retailers benefit because customers are presented with more items that they are likely to purchase, which will increase revenue.[25]

CHRIS It's clear that AI can speed up many aspects of a business, from manufacturing, to content creation, to addressing consumers' wants and needs quickly.

AIMÉ Yes – in terms of an emphasis on speed, AI can help organizations address the balance between short-term and long-term goals.

CHAPTER 8

Understanding

Revealing and mastering deep insights

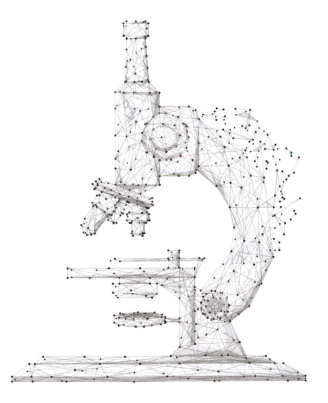

CHRIS We just talked about how AI can improve speed. Equally important is how it can improve the understanding of your customers, employees and marketplace.

AIMÉ On the surface, understanding seems to be a no-brainer, but when you think about how to come to an understanding, you realize the complexity of the subject. Machine learning, which we talked about earlier, is the ability of machines to learn new things without receiving specific programming. Think about that – a computer learning, improving, coming to conclusions and predicting without intervention from human beings. By using data gained from the environment, machines can change their conclusions and the way they operate.

Using machine learning, AI systems are solving the problems of recognizing objects and speech, translating languages, playing games and extrapolating based upon image and video recognition. However, each of these requires systems tailored for the specific task at hand – general AI does not yet exist. This is because the subject of intelligence is complicated. As an article in AxiomZen stated, 'you can't just pour raw data into AI and expect something meaningful to come out – this kind of AI simply doesn't exist yet'.[1]

CHRIS That's interesting. To demonstrate the complexity of understanding, let's look at the conversation between two human beings in the same room.

Human-to-human interaction

AIMÉ I'm enamoured by human-to-human interaction. Tell me more.

CHRIS When two humans are communicating, consider all the dynamics and dimensions that are engaged. You've got sight, tonality, sentence structure, voice inflection, body language, position of the eyes, historical context, affinity of the two speakers, pronunciation, emotional state of the speakers, the intent of the communication, education, the interpersonal dynamic and an infinite number of other variables. Communication and understanding are not necessarily simple.

AIMÉ That explains why emails or text messages are so often misunderstood. Sarcasm and humour often depend on body language and tone of voice, which are not communicated in emails. This can lead to misunderstandings of the intent of the communication.

CHRIS When you add the factor of different cultures and upbringings to the interaction, you have set the stage for interpersonal disconnects.

AI expands understanding

AIMÉ AI can expand understanding, enabling true connections even when done over a great distance or time. It's now possible to create deep, lasting connections.

CHRIS Deeper understanding allows for deeper connections.

AIMÉ That's important for businesses, because they can identify individuals and groups who are interested in their products and service and avoid those who are disinterested.

CHRIS A business could display ads only when a consumer was able to understand the message, wanted the product or service, and the locale was appropriate. Great experiences are amplified by the appropriate location, contextualized and individualized.

According to Juniper Research, ad spend for real-time bidding networks will reach $42 billion globally by the year 2021. A study by Boxever done in November 2016 found that almost 80 per cent of the senior marketers in the US believe consumers are ready for AI, and most of those marketers were excited about chatbots.[2,3]

Machine learning is being used to improve the targeting of ads, because they use AI to identify customers and serve ads that are relevant. These algorithms don't just display ads for products previously viewed; they infer other products to recommend, the timing of the ads and where they are placed.[4]

All these trends indicate that understanding the actual needs and wants of consumers results in placing more relevant advertisements, which increases profits.

AIMÉ That's very true, but let's look at the flip side; as great as this is, we should be mindful of the algorithm paradox. This happens when you only introduce products and services to people who have shown an affinity for them, so you wind up missing out on introducing new or unexpected things.

Now that we've deconstructed understanding to an extent, and found that it is in fact quite difficult to understand, let's delve into different aspects of how AI can improve understanding with some real-world examples.

How AI improves understanding

CHRIS As we've discussed, understanding humans and communication includes knowing body language and being able to perform facial recognition, gait analysis, eye tracking and so forth.

AIMÉ One company I'm fond of is Modiface, which provides unique customized experiences that utilize AR and AI for marketing beauty products.

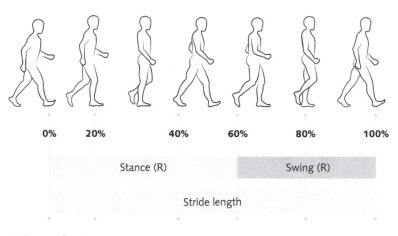

0%	20%	40%	60%	80%	100%

Stance (R)	Swing (R)

Stride length

Gait analysis
www.apdm.com/wp-content/uploads/2015/05/Whitepaper.pdf

CHRIS Yes, their technology is embedded into several native OS systems and can be downloaded through apps as well. Using augmented reality, people can see how they look by virtually simulating makeup on images of their face on their smartphone or tablet.

Their technology is based on research from Stanford University, and is one of the most precise facial video tracking systems in the world. AI comes into play because their highly accurate 3D facial feature tracks precise movements and expressions. The software understands 68 parameters that include the iris size and location, lips, eyes, head pose and other facial characteristics. The Modiface technology is embedded in smart mirrors that can analyse the human face and body.[5]

AIMÉ This is a glimpse of how AI can be used in smart homes and stores in the very near future. Smart mirrors will be common in bathrooms and dressing rooms to let consumers virtually 'try on' different clothes and makeup. Suppose someone is trying out makeup using a smart mirror in their bathroom. They choose different colours, shades and styles using a selector. When they find one they like they can physically apply it to their face; if they don't own that brand or style already, they can tell the smart mirror to order it, and may even be able to have the products delivered within a few hours.[6]

CHRIS For now, this technology is being used for commercial applications to market makeup and clothing. In the future, applications such as this could be used for body language analysis to enhance communication. I foresee an app that helps people learn about themselves to prepare for interviews and presentations. There are obviously many ways this kind of product could be used commercially and by individuals to improve themselves.

AIMÉ Yes, that's pretty intriguing. I'm imagining that someone with a job interview could rehearse in front of a smart mirror to understand their weak points and improve their game. The mirror could tell them that they appear to be nervous and give them hints on how to correct it.

Take this even further. By using AI to evaluate multiple data sources, such as the weather service, a person's calendar and a list of local social events, a 'smart closet' could recommend clothes that are appropriate for the forecast, where the person will be going that day and events in the local area.[7]

Combining a variety of products such as smart TVs, smart mirrors, smart thermostats, smart locks and alarm systems, smart security cameras and smart kitchen appliances together with a smart home hub creates an integrated smart home or smart apartment (and smart offices and so on). These systems all build an integrated understanding of the habits and desires of the inhabitants to provide an environment tailored to their specific needs.[8]

AI benefits communication

CHRIS AI can benefit many other forms of communication. Take, for instance, natural language processing and generation. Recently, Kristian Hammond told an audience at EmTech MIT:

> Language by itself is miraculous and uniquely human. You can teach a dog things; crows use tools; beavers use dams. There is no other creature that uses language the way we use language. Although machines use words, they struggle with language.[9]

Hammond, who is the Professor of Computer Science at Northwestern University and a co-founder of Narrative Science, created a product called Quill. This software transforms data into human-sounding intelligent narrative.[10] Quill analyses data, creates narrative then creates a story around it. As a case in point, using Quill, companies can automate the process of writing quarterly regulatory reports, which enables people to spend time reviewing them instead of creating them. The technology can also be used to enhance customer engagement and improve operational efficiency.[11]

AIMÉ That's a magnificent illustration of AI helping to aid understanding. Quill scours data, and each data exploration centres on two questions that are key to creating a story. What is being talked about, and what needs to be known about it. Quill then produces results that are communicated in a way that is easy for humans to understand.[12]

CHRIS This reminds me of a use case where the hospitality industry is using AI to aid a business's understanding of their customers. With that, they can deliver incredible service seamlessly.

Suppose Melissa wants to go to New York with her friends for her 30th birthday. She jumps on her smartphone and searches for one of her favourite hotels in midtown New York. She's attracted to the high-tech amenities it offers, such as Mobile Key and Mobile Check in. The app quickly tells her that a room is available, but the phone rings and Melissa accepts the call and forgets to book the room. A few days later, while on Facebook, she sees a paid search ad reminding her to book the room. Melissa reserves the room and lets all her friends know that the trip is on.

Fast-forward to the week before her trip. Melissa receives an email inviting her to use her mobile app to check in to the room. She takes advantage of the check-in service. On the day of the trip, she walks into the hotel and receives a push notification welcoming her back, and reminding her that she can proceed directly to her room. The message includes her room number, and informs that her she can unlock the door with her mobile app. She goes directly to her room without stopping at the front desk in the lobby.

Melissa uses the app on her mobile phone to unlock the door and gets access to her room. Once inside, she turns on the TV and receives a personalized message welcoming her and inviting her to log on to the hotel website for a list of curated experiences. She looks through the list and buys tickets to the Knicks game, and spends the weekend with her closest friends cheering the Knicks to victory.

AIMÉ That's a fine example of a hotel using data to improve its understanding of its customer. This also showcases some of the challenges of understanding and addressing the three major pain points of many businesses.

The first difficulty is that the data is siloed, which means it is stored in different databases on different systems, and not always shared between departments in an organization. Second, the data lacks structure and, third, the data is not actionable.

In this case, the hotel leveraged AI to compile a unified view of the customer. This enables the hotel to process high-velocity and high-volume data in real time. They process petabytes of data in real time to inform experience as it's happening.[13]

Healthcare applications

CHRIS In healthcare, for instance, Ada, which is a London and Berlin health tech startup, markets what they call a 'personal health companion and telemedicine app'. Patients tell the app their symptoms, which then offers them information on possible causes and does a symptom assessment. If circumstances warrant, Ada recommends a follow-up consultation with a real medical professional.[14]

The artificial intelligence engine was trained over several years using actual cases combined with a medical database with information about conditions, symptoms and diagnoses.[15]

AIMÉ Another example is Samsung's Know You Again AI glasses, which have been combined with augmented reality glasses capabilities. This gives people with dementia or Alzheimer's the ability to be prompted with a heads-up display showing not only who is approaching them but some key facts about the person they are looking at and perhaps components of the last conversation they may have had. This is an instance of artificial intelligence creating innovative and meaningful experiences.[16]

Understanding customers

CHRIS The need to understand customers is nothing new; it's just become more sophisticated. If you look back historically, even the sellers in marketplaces in ancient times had awareness of the behaviours, habits and desires of their customers. These vendors would hone their pitch depending on the context. Perhaps they'd sell refreshing watermelon on hot days, fish on Fridays and fresh bakery during special events.

Now the conversation has become more advanced because using AI we can adaptively learn customers' wants, behaviours and needs to create better, more personalized experiences.

This understanding can be seen in supermarkets, which may all seem to be the same in many respects because they are designed with an understanding of human behaviour in mind. Fresh products, such as fruits and vegetables, are usually placed near the front of the store, because buying fresh foods makes people feel good and less guilty about buying a less healthy selection later on.[17]

To fully understand the customer requires vast amounts of information spanning years, locations, businesses and the virtual and physical worlds. In a simple case, Amazon could give customized results based on your Google searches, or, to add complexity, by knowing what stores you visited this week and what you bought and examined. This information is often stored in different databases by separate businesses, making centralized access difficult.

One of the problems services such as Adobe Experience Cloud solves is de-siloing data based on geofencing, behaviour and other criteria to provide insights for deeply personalized experiences aimed precisely at individual customers.

The data feedback loop

By understanding behaviour and providing a meaningful, AI-driven experience, businesses sustain customer loyalty, effectively keeping the competition at bay. In today's fast-moving, constantly changing world, orchestrating virtually instant, gratifying, helpful and precisely delivered experiences is the way to achieve and execute marketplace success.

AIMÉ This brings us to our next topic of discussion – performance, which focuses on measurement and optimization.

CHAPTER 9

Performance

Measurement and optimization

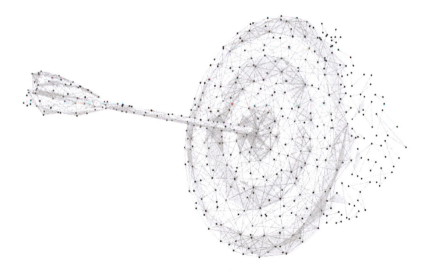

CHRIS Performance is essentially an evaluation of how well something is functioning with the goal of improving – optimizing – the accuracy and supporting decision making. This is distinct from speed, understanding, experimentation and results.

There are three steps to performance. First, identify the goal of your AI solution and define your key performance indicators (KPIs). This is done at the onset of your initiative, although changes and course corrections can be made at key milestones. Second, track and measure the performance against your KPIs. Third, based on the results according to your KPIs, you then go back to the second step to optimize your solution.

Key performance indicators

KPIs are measurements that demonstrate the effectiveness of achieving objectives. These allow businesses and teams to determine if they are getting results.[1]

AIMÉ Performance measurement and optimization can be defined as the process of collecting, analysing or reporting information regarding the performance of an individual, group, organization, system or component. These can involve studying processes and strategies within organizations, or studying engineering processes, parameters and phenomena, to see whether outputs are in line with what was intended or should have been achieved. There are endless amounts

1	**2**	**3**
Define KPIs	Track & measure KPI	Optimize

Three steps

of theories, principles and academic laws about performance that have been codified, but many times they are blindly rolled out, which sometimes ends up missing the overall point.

A recent approach called Design Thinking is now making its way across organizations as a successful methodology to explore and solve not only design/software problems but also complex business performance problems – this general notion of having a hyper-focused approach on measuring and optimizing for peak performance is relevant when it comes to AI solutions as well.

Strategy and tactics

Within the SUPER framework, performance measures and optimizes how well the AI solution is achieving the goals on a tactical and

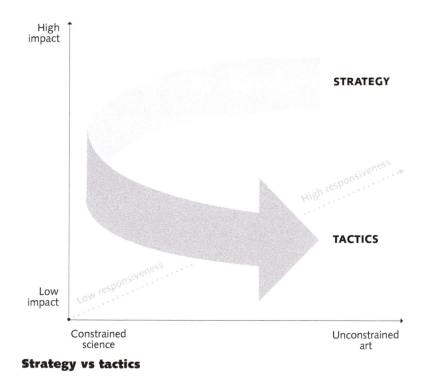

Strategy vs tactics

strategic level. A couple of thousand years ago, in THE ART OF WAR, military strategist Sun Tzu wrote, 'Strategy without tactics is the slowest route to victory. Tactics without strategy is the noise before defeat.' What that means, and it is still true today, is that strategies are the long-term goals of a business and the plan on how to achieve them. Tactics are the steps needed to achieve the strategy. Tactics are components of a strategy.[2]

All businesses will, in one way or another, have opportunities to use AI, because all organizations constantly need to become more intelligent to compete. However, if your business just puts together an AI strategy, it won't get very far. You'll be more successful if you build a business strategy that takes advantage of AI.

CHRIS To that point, I recently talked to a friend who used to be a Formula One driver about how AI is being employed for performance purposes in races. Each car has over 200 sensors gathering data points as the cars race. These sensors record how the engine is working, the grip of the tyres, temperatures and so on. Pierre d'Imbleval, Chief Information Officer for Renault Sport Formula One Team, said, 'Artificial intelligence would be so important during a race. We need help to take the best decisions that have to be taken during each lap time.' Using that information, the sports cars are optimized so they perform even better. But this doesn't just mean modifying the car itself; AI could predict the optimum time to change the tyres at the pit stop, for instance.[3,4]

Technology from Microsoft is the power behind this initiative. Azure Machine Learning, which is their AI framework in their cloud, is used to help predict the measurement and optimization of car configurations. This uses Microsoft Cloud and Azure Stream Analytics and works with Renault's supercomputer to test using 3D virtual car designs.[5]

AIMÉ That's an example of how AI is measuring performance and providing insights for optimization and competitive advantage on both a tactical and strategic level.

If that wasn't thought-provoking enough, now they are using Microsoft HoloLens to visualize things like airflow over the car. HoloLens was originally conceived as a workplace product, useful for collaborative working, for training and for education. It's also been used to display architecture, auto prototyping, medical training and other similar applications. Combined with AI, the possibilities for improving creativity are limitless.[6,7]

CHRIS Fanuc's Gakushu Learning Software (*Gakushu* means learning) is embedded in manufacturing robots to speed up operations and is intended to accelerate deep learning. These robots learn manufacturing tasks by collecting and storing data, then they adjust to real-time conditions. After the learning process is completed, the trained robots operate autonomously. Measurements of the performance led to the conclusion that this sped up the spot welding tasks by 15 per cent.[8]

Measure to fine tune success

AIMÉ Measurement is vital to know if the project is succeeding, but it can be somewhat of a polarizing notion because there is often a fear of being judged as a failure. But, these are not failures – they are opportunities for optimization. Even the KPIs themselves may need to be optimized based on the results of measurements and statistics in the real world.

CHRIS Instead, ask yourself questions if the stats and outcomes aren't rolling to your KPIs. The answers to these questions may introduce opportunities for AI to overcome the barriers.

AIMÉ And ask questions such as: Have you given it enough time? Are there broader contextual marketplace dynamics that weren't foreseeable? Should you re-examine and evolve your KPIs? Did the product underperform for technical reasons, such as the hardware is unable to support the performance or the network too slow?

CHRIS Also, look at your marketing. Was the marketing aimed at the appropriate audience? Was the marketing properly funded? Are you measuring correctly? Can you correlate the attribution?

AIMÉ The point is that measurement and KPIs must be examined holistically. You must understand the confidence level of your statistics. The environment must be taken into consideration. Is the quality of the data as pure as you believe?

CHRIS Yes, measurement is important, but the conclusions you make based on measurements can't be looked at within an echo chamber. The world can be complex, and a few measurements don't always take that complexity into account.

AIMÉ Indeed. Upon analysis, you could find you need more measurements or the ones you have are imprecise or wrongly targeted. Remember, measurements are just data points and are not conclusions. You form conclusions based on data points – measurements – and if these are incorrect or insufficient, your conclusions will be wrong.

Data sources

CHRIS I remember an old saying: 'No battle plan ever survives contact with the enemy.' Your plan needs to be flexible because the complexity of the real world and marketplace is always evolving, requiring continuous adaption. That's why the optimization step is so important.

Understanding the quality of your source data is critical to the success of your AI project. According to *McKinsey Quarterly*, 'A well-constructed provenance model can stress-test the confidence for a go/no-go decision and help management decide when to invest in improving a critical data set.'[9]

AIMÉ Do you know what provenance means? It's where or when something originated. In the case of data, you want to know where the data came from and when it arrived, so you can judge its reliability. You must look at each bit of data and establish its pedigree. Was the data entered by the user? Did it come from an IoT device? Was the information gathered from social media or was it transactional?[10]

CHRIS You've got it, Aimé. It's vital to understand the source of information. You don't want to base decisions on data that's suspect. That can lead to incorrect assessments of performance, and then you'll find yourself optimizing for the wrong thing.

Now, let's look at the importance of performance in manufacturing. In many cases this is where the rubber hits the road. In the quest to reduce costs and improve efficiency, the opportunity for AI is to help factories forecast demand, predict capacity, foresee equipment failures and so on.

Industry 4.0

AIMÉ You mean the so-called Industry 4.0 initiative?

CHRIS Precisely, and it's also been called the Fourth Industrial Revolution. Automating factories with robots and AI resolves a lot of the problems you mentioned. According to Volkhard Bregulla, Vice President of Global Manufacturing Industries at Hewlett Packard Enterprise:

> AI-enabled predictive maintenance allows manufacturers to achieve 60 per cent or more reduction in unscheduled system downtime, which dramatically reduces costs that accumulate across production downtime, part replacements and inventory.[11]

Additionally, 'Traditional industrial automation requires hundreds of hours to reprogram, making it very impractical to change how the task is performed.' Machine learning reduces or eliminates delays to reprogram industrial robots.[12]

By identifying KPIs for maintenance, supply chain, quality control and automation, for instance, is where AI can play a major role in measurement and optimization. Robots are already commonly used in manufacturing, but they need to be trained by humans to perform their functions. Deep-learning-enabled robots can learn how to do a task, then improve it over time.

One of the places where AI can truly help manufacturing is to automate the entire business process rather than individual tasks or components. To do this, a software robot is taught how a job is done on a job-by-job basis. These individual tasks are coordinated as a single, unified process. To monitor and control the whole process, managers – human beings – use a dashboard to see all the activities in one place.[13]

AIMÉ To take AI's impact on performance in manufacturing even further, look at 'cobots', collaborative robots that work together with human beings. This can increase productivity even more by making the collaboration between humans and machines more integrated, thus taking advantage of the strengths of each.[14]

Closer to home, iRobot is improving their Roomba robotic vacuum cleaner to map rooms, to then be able to identify and remember those rooms later. The robot can then adjust its cleaning habits depending on the room. This requires that the Roomba be able to chart out a room based upon a grid pattern and then segment all the different rooms and hallways. The robot must continually adjust its performance and optimize its path because homes are occupied and change constantly. People may move furniture around, drop clothing in the middle of the floor, or have mobile challenges such as pets and small children. Engineers at iRobot evaluate the performance of the robotic vacuum cleaners in the field and incorporate optimized results and improvements in the next version.[15]

Implications for farming

CHRIS The implications of AI for agriculture are impressive as well. Farming requires water, energy, manual labour, fertilizer and other resources. AI adds intelligence to farming. I like to refer to it as informative farming.

AIMÉ Today, farmers often irrigate crops in a field with volumes of water, blanket everything with pesticides and apply tremendous masses of fertilizer without much precision. Now, farmers are placing sensors in the soil in their fields to monitor the levels of water and nutrients in real time. Once the data has been compiled and analysed, it becomes possible to precisely control water, pesticides and fertilizer. By using that data, AI-enabled devices can pipe water only to where it is needed, spray pesticides directly on problem plants or areas, and fertilize precise locations instead of entire fields. The entire process requires constant monitoring of the performance of the solution, which leads to real-time optimization of farming.

CHRIS There is a huge opportunity to identify and handle diseases in plants before outbreaks occur and wipe out entire crops. In Tanzania, a team of researchers developed an AI system to identify diseases in plants using a technique known as transfer learning. Google's open AI product known as TensorFlow was used to build a library of 2,756 images of cassava leaves from plants. Once they had done that, the AI could identify a disease in the plants with 98 per cent accuracy.[16]

AIMÉ That reminds me of the AI-enhanced cucumber farm. It turns out that sorting cucumbers is difficult because each one has a slightly different colour, shape, quality, texture and freshness.

Makoto Koike explored this using machine learning to sort cucumbers on the family farm into nine different classes using TensorFlow. The system used deep learning, which consisted of training the system over the course of three months using 7,000 images, to recognize images and classify them. Up until that point, his mother had to spend up to eight hours a day sorting cucumbers, and afterwards this time was greatly reduced through the use of this measurement and optimization model.[17]

Impact on logistics

CHRIS If AI can have such a big impact on sorting cucumbers, imagine the effect it could have on global logistics, an industry that has traditionally been overwhelmed by the volume of data from the complexity of the global supply network. This problem is compounded by the need to integrate the quickly growing implementation of the internet of things, which produces a phenomenal amount of data in real time.

AIMÉ In logistics, there are many moving parts that must all work together, spanning multinational companies, numerous suppliers and service providers, each using vastly different equipment, databases and software.[18] Add to that is the complexity of different human languages, and quite often the records aren't even computerized.

'We expect that artificial intelligence, machine learning, corporate social responsibility and cost-to-serve analytics will all drive significant shifts in supply chain strategies within the next decade,' reports Gartner Research VP Noha Tohamy, the chief analyst on the report.[19]

IBM and The Weather Channel are working together on a project called Deep Thunder, which uses machine learning to help understand severe weather and its impact on industry. Deep Thunder uses IBM Watson to examine over 100 terabytes of

2010–2015	2015–2020	2020–2025	2030–2035

Autonomous guided vehicles (yards)

Autonomous cranes

Mobile robots

Drones

Autonomous ships

Truck platooning

Autonomous trucks

Autonomous rail

Self-driving cars

Autonomous logistics in upstream management
© Richard Martin 2010

data every day to produce 'far more reliable weather forecasts, including the kind of location-specific information about impacts of storms, hurricanes and typhoons that is vital for supply chains to know'.[20]

CHRIS Another example of performance enhanced by AI is Rolls-Royce launching R² Data Labs. These connect people all over their company and enable them to use data and AI in order to find insights and unlock more value for their customers. They use machine learning to analyse the huge volume of data.[21]

GE is creating a 'digital twin' of every jet engine they manufacture, allowing them to monitor the performance of the engines from the ground in real time, including while the plane is in flight. Using this technology, GE can predict when engines will need repair and know from real-life data how each engine is being used.[22]

Anthony Dean, Head of Combustion Systems at General Electric's Global Research Center in New York, said:

> With the twin...I can learn that the pilot is a cowboy and pushes the engine. The fuel burns we see will be different with different pilots. The digital twin remembers every one of those events. You can start to separate the fleet. Each engine has a different life experience.[23]

AIMÉ It's amazing to see how AI is affecting performance strategically and tactically by constantly measuring and optimizing products, services and the AI model itself.

CHRIS Right on. That's how AI is going to help businesses, humanity and make the world a better place.

CHAPTER 10

Experimentation

Actionable curiosity

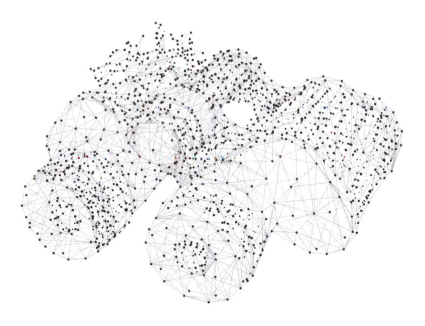

CHRIS Experimentation is not done for experimentation's sake; rather, it's aimed at resolving actionable problems. When we speak of experimentation and actionable curiosity within the SUPER framework, there are two aspects – curiosity can be built into the AI strategy or it can be built into the AI model itself.

The key to experimentation is beginning with a business problem, something actionable. You then use curiosity to work out possible solutions and experiment to validate if those solutions solve the problem. We call this actionable curiosity.

AIMÉ There have been many examples of humankind using curiosity and imagination to solve real-world problems. Even before AI and computers, humans have always had an ability to resolve problems in impressive and often dramatic ways. Look at Roman aqueducts and the SpaceX programme, separated by 2,000 years, yet connected by a common thread of people using their inherent curiosity and imagination to solve seemingly unsolvable real-world problems.

The Roman aqueducts

CHRIS That's true – the aqueducts in ancient Rome are one of the greatest and most useful inventions of all time. They had a real

| Water source | Inverted syphon | | Bridge over lower ground | Distribution |

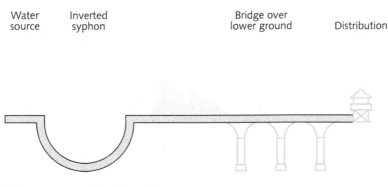

How an aqueduct works
https://science.howstuffworks.com/environmental/green-science/la-ancient-rome1.htm

problem to solve. Rome was growing fast and had a huge population for the time. Water is the limiting factor in the growth of any city. Without sufficient water, the population can't grow. Additionally, people become restive during times of drought and water shortages, which makes the issue even more urgent.[1]

Rome solved these problems by building aqueducts, which are basically canals designed to move water from mountain springs into a city where it can be used. Building aqueducts is not a simple thing that can be done easily and without forethought. Think about it – the challenges and complexity are daunting, especially without advanced technology.

But the problem was critical, and as Rome's population grew it became even more pressing. Of course, people have always dug trenches to move water into villages, fields and even towns and cities. That had been done since the beginning of agriculture, when it became necessary to channel water from rivers and streams into the fields to water crops. Out of necessity, the Romans were curious about how to solve their water problem. After years of experimentation and experience, they finally came up with the idea of building aqueducts to ship water long distances to Rome.

The effort to solve their problem was exceedingly difficult, to say the least, but they didn't really have a choice. For the city of Rome to increase its population, and to be resistant to drought, they needed a regular, safe supply of water. They had to move water from mountain springs many miles away, and cross natural barriers such as rivers, streams and mountains. Each aqueduct began in a mountain spring and transported the water on a channel or in lead pipes. If there was a stream or river in the path, a bridge was built out of stone. If there was a mountain in the way, a tunnel was dug through the mountain. All of this was done without the benefit of pumps; water flowed down to the city because of gravity.

Think about the bureaucracy needed to make this vast enterprise happen. Generally, wealthy Romans paid for aqueducts out of their own pockets or citizens were levied special taxes, and this financing had to be organized and focused. Sometimes merchants donated material goods, such as pipes, and other times they might give money.

Thousands of individual workers and their managers had to be hired, fed, clothed and housed during the construction. Tools had to be created to dig tunnels, build bridges and lay pipes and channels. It was a massive undertaking and would be difficult even today.

AIMÉ Imagine being the engineer organizing that effort, without phones, computers, email or heavy equipment. Everything was done without any modern technology such as explosives, heavy equipment, trucks, computers or anything of that nature. That's an astonishing accomplishment.

CHRIS Experimentation had to be done to determine the best way to build each part of the aqueduct. On top of that, the effort needed to be supported with logistics, meaning temporary cities had to be built, regular supplies delivered, and so forth.

The problem led to curiosity and experimentation and they resolved it by building aqueducts. Without a problem, the solution would never have been tried or even needed.

AIMÉ Aqueducts weren't created because the Romans *could* – they were created to solve a real social problem.

CHRIS To that point, another take on it is, once the problem is solved, you need to define the next problem to continue progress. Perhaps the Apollo moon project didn't live up to its full potential because it didn't have a problem to solve or the problem wasn't clearly defined or promoted. The original problem was solved; we got to the moon first, but after that was accomplished, Apollo was completed in the minds of the public and without a clearly defined mission, the project essentially stopped.

SpaceX

AIMÉ That's a compelling notion. As I said before, aqueducts are a spectacular example of curiosity and experimentation used to solve a problem. Looking at modern times, the SpaceX programme was created to solve a different, but still very complex problem.

Lifting materials from the surface of Earth into space is expensive and requires a lot of energy. A big portion of the expense is that traditionally most of the rocket is discarded after every launch. Hundreds of millions of dollars is thrown away and not recovered. Each launch of Apollo costs $1.16 billion, adjusted for inflation, to lift 310,000 pounds into low Earth orbit or 107,100 pounds to the moon. That's the equivalent of nine full-grown elephants.[2]

Even in the space shuttle programme, the massive boosters fell into the ocean to be destroyed and were not reused.

That's the problem that needed to be solved. SpaceX resolved to address the issue by creating boosters that could land back on earth, allowing them to be reused over and over. This lowers the cost of boosting materials into space by several times and has the side effect that launches can occur more often. This is because new boosters don't need to be manufactured for each launch; they just need to be refurbished, tested and checked out and then reused. When all is said and done, the Falcon Heavy lift system will be able to deliver 35,000 pounds to the moon or 140,700 pounds to low Earth orbit at $90 million per launch.[3]

As with the aqueducts, once the problem was identified, a solution could be found. An entire infrastructure needed to be created from scratch, complete with engineers, workers, manufacturers and an entire logistics chain to supply everything.

CHRIS SpaceX puts AI to good use to land its reusable boosters back on earth. The solution solves a 'convex optimization problem', which means to consider all possible answers to the question of how to land the rocket without running out of fuel.[4]

Actionable curiosity

AIMÉ People with more curiosity tend to be more inquisitive and open to new experiences. They seek out novel, exciting and thought-provoking things and grow bored with routine day-to-day activities. They are masters at creating new ideas and tend to be tolerant of ambiguity. These kinds of people easily handle complexity and use their curiosity to find simple solutions for complex problems.[5]

Actionable curiosity is all about ideation, which means to give yourself permission to be curious, and then to use that curiosity to embrace workable solutions to problems. Intelligence alone is not enough; that intelligence must be directed towards goals by actionable curiosity. Albert Einstein said, 'I have no special talent. I am only passionately curious.'

Currently, reinforcement learning is used to train most artificial intelligences by rewarding them when they achieve something that moves them towards a goal. This is a useful technique to teach AI-specific things, such as how to optimally build a car in an assembly line. However, for machines to operate autonomously without instructions, they must be curious.[6]

CHRIS That's great, Aimé, and I have an example. The folks at Google were curious about whether they could reduce the energy bills at their data centres. In 2014 those centres consumed 4,402,836 MWh of electricity, which is the same amount used by 366,903 US households. They were curious and asked themselves if AI could be used to find a solution.

They decided to experiment and designed neural networks that controlled 'about 120 variables in the data centers', including 'the fans and the cooling systems and so on, and windows and other things'. Google used DeepMind AI to reduce their power usage by 15 per cent. This was possible because people were curious, willing to experiment, and then designed an AI strategy to address the problem.[7]

AI models

AIMÉ Let's chat a little more about how curiosity is getting built into AI models. There are several types of AI, but for this discussion I'd like to focus on five of them because they are the most pertinent for a discussion about curiosity: reinforcement; supervised; unsupervised; transfer; and semi-supervised.

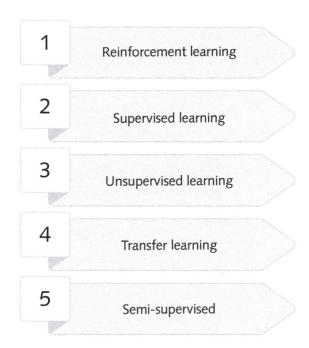

1 Reinforcement learning

2 Supervised learning

3 Unsupervised learning

4 Transfer learning

5 Semi-supervised

The five AI models

CHRIS Yes, but of course there are many more methods or types of AI.

AIMÉ These five kinds of AI learning are those that embed active curiosity, plus a few variations on the same theme.

CHRIS The first is reinforcement learning, in which the computer is trying to make specific decisions by being placed into an environment in which it trains itself by trial and error. Learning from experience, the machine captures the best possible way to make accurate decisions.

Andrew Ng, VP and Chief Scientist of Baidu, Co-Chairman and Co-Founder of Coursera and an Adjunct Professor at Stanford University, compares this to how you might train a puppy. When the dog does something desirable you reward it, and when it does something undesirable you don't reward it. After some time, the dog understands what it's supposed to do because it's been rewarded for taking the right path.[8] Reinforcement learning works very well to solve a specific, known problem.

AIMÉ The second type is supervised learning, which you could compare to a teacher supervising the learning process. The teacher understands the correct answers, the AI system keeps making predictions on its training data set, and any wrong answers are corrected by the teacher. When the AI can perform the task acceptably, the learning is done.

CHRIS In unsupervised learning, there is no correct answer and no teacher involved. The AI figures out on its own what's interesting in the data.[9]

AIMÉ The fourth kind of AI that is useful to our discussion is called transfer learning. This is a machine learning method where what was developed for one task is reused to begin a second one. You might have used supervised learning to train your AI to recognize certain kinds of objects in a set of 10,000 photographs. If you had another project that involved photographs, you might use the learning that the AI had already accomplished to start your new project.

In the fifth type, called semi-supervised machine learning, the AI system is given labelled data to help the algorithm and give it a start, and once it has achieved a certain level of proficiency it is trained on other, unlabelled information.[10]

CHRIS Andrew Ng stated, 'I would say, out of all of these categories, supervised learning is the one that's creating clear value. Some of these other categories I feel like the algorithms and the thinking and how they take it to market are still in the early stage.'[11]

AIMÉ In each of these five models, AI uses curiosity, the desire to find out the solution, to build understanding.

CHRIS A great example of an application that uses imagination and curiosity is Adobe Project Scene Stitch. This AI solution acts in a similar way to a content aware fill but looks through a large number of other images to find graphic elements that would look good in the image.[12]

Ultimately, we use AI's curiosity and experimentation to solve business problems. The 'north star' for experimentation should be invention. With that goal in mind, there is a component of bravery that's needed. Often, the team will be exploring uncharted territory.

AIMÉ That's true. If you are not willing to have failures, you can't succeed.

CHRIS The only limit to AI is imagination. You must not only be willing to think out of the box, but you must also get rid of the box.

CHAPTER 11

Results

Business transformation

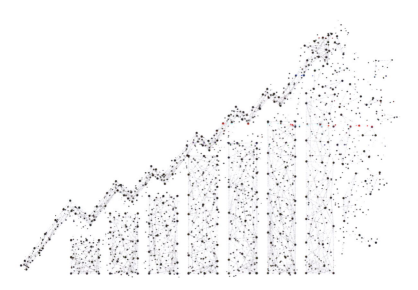

CHRIS The result of AI is business change. For business to survive, they must transform digitally and organizationally. But companies need to get started to achieve the results of AI. According to Forbes, 80 per cent of enterprises are investing in AI.[1]

When you are creating your AI strategy, your results will impact your product, your ROI and your business. You can't think of it in isolation. Your AI solution will result in a greater ability to compete at multiple levels and will transform your organization. This is the true value of AI.

At the end of the day, results are what it's all about. While developing an AI strategy, the results don't stop at just one project, product or service. Those results must contribute to the overall digital, business transformation and the bottom line.

Enabled products and services

AIMÉ Let's look at the results of AI-enabled products and services. Chris, we've talked about the Roomba AI vacuuming solution before. I think that's a great example to illustrate what we are discussing.

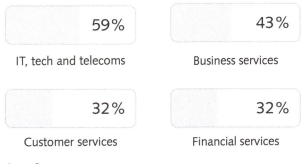

59%	43%
IT, tech and telecoms	Business services
32%	32%
Customer services	Financial services

Industries that expect to see the greatest impact from AI

Contact analysis

Object classification

Geospatial image classification

Automated geophysical detection

Image text query

Social media content distribution

Predictive maintenance

Scalable patient data processing

Static image classification and tagging

Algorithmic trading strategy

0 $2500

Artificial intelligence revenue
Top 10 use cases, world markets 2025
Tractica

CHRIS Yes, we did talk about it. One of my least favourite chores is vacuuming, and the Roomba product solved that nicely for me. I got one a few years ago and was thrilled that it could vacuum the entire house without my intervention. Our dog likes playing with it too!

It was like magic. The little robot just travelled around the house, and I didn't have to do anything except empty its dustbin occasionally. How wonderful is that?

AIMÉ Yes, that's showing the results of AI to create a product line, because obviously the concept won't work without AI. The little robot must create a map of your home to understand where to vacuum. Keep in mind that map is constantly changing as people move about, furniture changes position and pets wander around.[2]

CHRIS Roomba is a terrific example of how AI resulted in the success of a new company based on a product line of robotic vacuum cleaners. Each new generation of the concept builds on the previous one, adding new, more advanced AI to make vacuuming an even easier task for the consumer.

Robotics

AIMÉ: As an aside, when people talk about robotics they think of anthropomorphized human-like machines. In reality, most robots are purpose-built to sizes and shapes specific to a task. Take RobotWaiter, which accepts orders for food via mobile phone and then brings the food to the hungry customer on a tray. The robot is a cart on wheels and doesn't have any resemblance to the human form. That avoids the Uncanny Valley aspect, which is the uncomfortable feeling that people get when a robot appears to be almost human, as written up in 1970 by the Japanese roboticist Masahiro Mori.[3,4]

CHRIS In fact, the point here is that AI creates new products. It's not only going to enhance products, services and projects, it's going to create new products. Look at what AI is doing in the medical field, inspiring new, meaningful products that extend and save lives and improve the quality of care.

AIMÉ Yes. I'm inspired by what Zebra Medical Vision is doing with radiology. They've created an AI Radiology assistant, and for $1 per scan a radiologist can get expert advice to help with diagnosis.[5] The results are better medical care at an affordable cost.

But let's not forget how AI can help with the product itself and the 'surround sound' (the things around the product) in terms of processes, marketing and manufacturing. AI will transform supergrid logistics, logistics marketplaces, de-stressing the supply chain, on-demand delivery, shareconomy logistics, personalized marketing, to name a few.[6]

The effect on return on investment

CHRIS AI is obviously having a big impact on products themselves, both new and existing, but it's having an even larger effect on return on investment (ROI). According to recent studies, the effect of AI is being felt across multiple industries, such as finance, transportation, healthcare, travel and automotive. Early adopters of AI are seeing positive growth on their bottom line. Retailers are using robots driven by AI in warehouses, consulting firms use it to build reports for their clients, hospitals are experimenting with AI to provide better healthcare and chatbots are improving customer service in all industries.[7]

AIMÉ There are two approaches to applying AI strategy to the bottom line, either a growth strategy or cost savings strategy. According to Teradata, 60 per cent of decision makers believe that AI can be used to automate repetitive processes and tasks, 50 per cent said AI delivers new strategic insights, and 49 per cent claimed AI can automate areas of knowledge work, which reduces the need for human resources.[8]

CHRIS Yes, and I found it striking that 46 per cent of those surveyed said it will enable them to innovate faster and find new market opportunities before the competition.

AI enabling growth

AIMÉ All of these come down to AI enabling growth, saving costs or both. An article in *Forbes* stated that, by 2035, AI could potentially increase productivity by 40 per cent and will increase economic growth by 1.7 per cent across 16 industries.[9]

In healthcare, AI chatbots will, according to Juniper Research, produce annual cost savings that will exceed $3.6 billion globally by 2022. Chatbots save costs by allowing patients to access care more easily and efficiently without the use of human beings.[10]

CHRIS We must remember that new products are also growth strategies because they enable businesses to enter new markets or enlarge their presence in existing areas.

AIMÉ On the flip side, by improving efficiencies or cutting costs, those businesses that implement AI solutions directly improve their ROI. As a case in point, L'Occitane increased mobile sales by 15 per cent using heat maps combined with AI to improve their process. Earth Fare boosted their year-on-year sales by using AI to create promotional recommendations for category managers. Amazon offers Prime members the option to complete their purchases using the AI in Alexa Echo to make recommendations.[11]

CHRIS Accenture Strategy research estimates that the digital economy represents 22.5 per cent of the world economy, and that companies that have taken advantage of digital disruption have made significant gains in terms of growth, profits and high market capitalizations. They also stated that 'digital's ability to unlock value is far from being fully exploited'.[12]

AIMÉ Those companies that do more to take advantage of the possibilities of digitalization, and specifically AI, will have a significant competitive advantage over those that are slower to leverage the digital economy. When combined with other digitalization trends such as the internet of things, SaaS, the cloud and so forth, most businesses will be unrecognizable. Those organizations that don't transform in all probability will not exist in the near future.

Business transformation

CHRIS Let's talk about the broader changes resulting from the impact of AI in business transformation.

AIMÉ This is a thought-provoking topic, with broader implication than just digital transformation.

CHRIS You're right. But before we get into that, let's define digital transformation, business transformation and innovation. These terms are frequently misunderstood and are often used interchangeably, but they actually have very different meanings.

Digital transformation is the change caused using digital technology, which is enabled by new types of innovation and creativity instead of just enhancing and supporting traditional ones.

Business transformation, on the other hand, is a strategy of change management to align the people, processes and technology of a company to its strategy and vision.

Innovation refers to making something new or changing an existing product, service or idea. It is the act of introducing those new ideas, devices or methods. Daniel Newman, principal analyst, said, 'Innovations drive changes and make them a reality.'[13]

Businesses use innovation to fuel digital transformation, which results in business transformation. AI is foundational to all three, and for your business to survive and prosper AI must be an integral component of your overarching strategy.

Digital verticals

AIMÉ As we've discussed, AI is across all digital verticals: the internet of things, the industrial internet of things, the internet of medical things, the cloud, and everything else. AI is foundational to them all.

CHRIS In fact, it is useless to have a digital or business transformation strategy without AI involved.

AIMÉ It is without question that AI is going to have game-changing results for products, ROI and businesses. There will be a need for AI investments, but the end game is business survival. The question now is where to start and where to focus your energy.

PART 3

The AI future

CHAPTER 12

Where to start

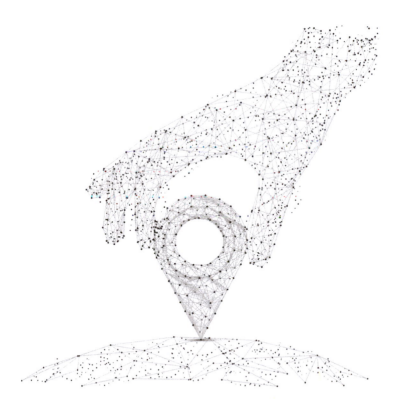

AIMÉ The most difficult question to answer when starting an AI project is to determine where to begin. The tendency is to jump straight into the technology without fully defining the problem or examining the market.

Defining the problem

Before starting, define what problem needs to be solved and who needs the solution. It's important to be very specific about your audience because these are the people who will purchase or use the product and who will define the requirements. What the end users need can be discovered using a variety of techniques, including market research, surveys and so on.

The definition of product has a broad meaning, which is different for business-to-business, business-to-customer, government, medical, internal, industrial and others. A product is the result of your project, and the customers are the users of the product. To illustrate, in an industrial application, the users are the manufacturers and in a business-to-customer product they are customers.

Without defining the problem and the market, it's likely the ROI will be weak and making sales will be difficult. Often, this is seen as technology for technology's sake, or doing it just because it can be done.

In other words, start with a business problem, an unused data set or survey the new AI techniques, which might identify a problem, a solution and a customer. Use the SUPER framework as a roadmap to get to the solution and to strategize the development of the AI project. As we referenced before, the SUPER framework is designed to support the business and brand strategy and is used in conjunction with them.

People

Process

Data   Technology

CHRIS To operationalize the SUPER framework, use the concept of people, process, data and technology. With people the concern is with building a team with the right skill set and organization. Processes deal with how the project is developed and the different methodologies available to achieve the goal. With data, have a data strategy and focus on quality not quantity, as well as accessibility. Finally, technology provides the software and hardware considerations on which to build the project.

The SUPER framework can be moulded and customized to fit the needs of any project. Just to be clear, this is a blueprint and is not intended as a straitjacket. Use the framework to enable progress, not to restrict your freedom of action.

AIMÉ Before we get into people, processes, data and technology, we should not underestimate the power of a shared vision or collective mindset. When any team or organization starts a project, it's all about alignment. While opinions may differ, the team and the organization need to be moving in the same direction towards agreed-upon goals.

Senior management must be aligned with the AI strategy and then there must be agreement across disciplines.

Change management

CHRIS If an organization is just starting with AI, which many are, change management strategy is very applicable. Change management helps build advocacy and a shared vision within organizations.

AIMÉ The thing that many leaders understand is people implement change and that you can't exclude people from the equation. Plans and processes are necessary but change often fails because the human side is not appropriately factored into the process.

CHRIS For an AI project to be successful, somebody must 'own' it. This doesn't imply that the project needs to be tightly managed; rather, one or more senior stakeholders in the business must support the project, its goals and the team. Where the project sits depends on how your company is organized.

AIMÉ There aren't hard and fast rules for how a company is organized. But, generally, a chief information officer (CIO) focuses on managing the infrastructure for business operations, while a chief technology officer (CTO) is responsible for technologies that grow the business externally.

CHRIS In other words, the CIO is generally in charge of internal IT and the CTO tends to be responsible for external technology and establishes the technical vision and technological development.

AIMÉ Larger companies may have both a CIO and a CTO, and even larger businesses can have more than one of each.

CHRIS Occasionally, especially in smaller organizations, IT is not represented at the highest level in the company. In these instances, the title will be something like vice president of management information services.

Embedded in the business

AIMÉ No matter how a company is organized, the AI team must be embedded within the business and not siloed. The Business

Dictionary defines the silo mentality as certain departments or sectors who do not want to share information with others in the same company.[1]

CHRIS If an AI team is isolated from the rest of the business, then their efficiency will be reduced, and they may not consider the needs of end users and stakeholders within the organization.

AIMÉ There also needs to be consideration of how data scientists and AI engineers work together. Are they working as one team or are there multiple teams? Do they work for the same organization? These and other questions must be addressed from the outset.

First, you need to define the role of the data scientist. Are they a business or domain expert, statistics expert, programming expert, data technology expert or a visualization and communications expert?[2]

CHRIS When starting an AI project, there are some questions that need to be asked to decide on the appropriate team.

AIMÉ One of the big decisions is deciding where the AI team sits within the organization. Is the project going to be run by the IT department, finance, marketing, or some other department?

CHRIS Of course, many areas of the business will be involved in the project. If you decide that your IT department is the appropriate owner, finance and marketing are probably still involved. Where the AI team sits relates to who has the ultimate responsibility for the project's staffing, assigning its resources and managing the process.

Deciding who owns the project is important, because each department has a certain type of affinity. IT tends to be focused on technology, marketing is focused on marketing efforts, and finance is focused on money. Whoever has responsibility for the project will tend to focus around their primary affinity.

AIMÉ Ownership can vary depending on the type of project. An AI project aimed primarily at providing reporting to the business might be best run by the finance department, because of their expertise in the area. A project that focuses on robotic AI solutions for industrial applications could be run by the logistics department.

CHRIS The primary owner of a project simply defines a person or group who is responsible for managing the resources and controlling the direction. Of course, team members from all areas of the business can and should be included on an AI project.

AIMÉ Generally, AI projects should be placed within the business side of the company, not the technology side. The business side tends to have a wider view, with a focus beyond the application or the hardware.

CHRIS A successful AI project includes a variety of people with multiple skill sets and varying responsibilities. One single person can't do everything; a team is required with several people, each with a distinct role to play.

Some of the skills that are needed include database design, data modelling, software engineering, and AI expertise specializing in deep learning or a similar technology. Additionally, most AI projects require team members from the business side who understand the functions or applications that are being developed or improved.

James Waterhouse, Head of Insight at Data Science at Sky Betting and Gaming, said:

> I don't think there's a perfect data scientist that bridges the skills you need to make things work at scale in real time on a massive platform all while understanding the business. Don't try to find a data scientist unicorn. I'd find three people and get them working together in a way that their skills rub off on each other.[3]

Business intelligence and data analysts who already understand the structure, purpose and layout of your data can be assigned to an AI project. They might need a certain amount of retraining to be able to put the data to use for artificial intelligence, but since they already understand the information specific to your business they have an advantage over new personnel.

You'll need experts who are skilled in AI algorithms as well as with coding skills. It's rare to find machine language experts who can also write code. Finding that combination in a single person can be very helpful to a project. If these skills are covered by more than one team member, then they need to coordinate very carefully and closely.

One of the most important actions to take is to educate the entire organization on the opportunities that AI makes available to the business. AI is a tool, and since people will be using that tool, they can provide valuable insights on how it can be put to use to make improvements.

Communicate throughout the business

AIMÉ To infuse AI into a company's culture, communicate throughout the business to increase awareness and acceptance of AI, and build an understanding of the purpose, terms and options available. Your business can also provide educational opportunities to bring members of your organization in all areas of your business up to speed on the concepts.[4]

The team can be based out of IT, which would be IT-centric, integrated between data science and IT or a specialized group with team members from throughout the business.[5]

CHRIS Highly intelligent and creative people tend to be involved in AI projects because they desire to be working on new and exciting technologies. These team members enjoy designing and creating new things, brainstorming and implementing new concepts that often have never been tried before.

Because of this, the selection of team members and appropriate project management methodology are crucial to the success of AI development teams. These types of individuals often require the freedom to innovate and don't appreciate or work well under strict project management rules.

AIMÉ That's why one of the most important decisions that will be made is determining which project management methodology is to be used. Of course, the organization could already be successfully using one of these methodologies, and that can be adapted for an AI project.

The options include waterfall, agile, scrum, kanban and a variety of others. Let's look at these four.

The waterfall methodology is a sequential, linear style, and is probably the best-known, because it's been in use for a long time. Often, a Gantt chart is used to aid in planning; this shows project milestones and other information in a bar graph format. This is a highly structured management style and tends to be very rigid. Each task shown on the Gantt chart must be done from beginning to end before the team can move on to the next one. Some tasks can be run in parallel, and the dependencies are built into the chart.

The advantage of this method is that it's easy to use and manage, discipline is enforced, documentation is required and progress reporting is built in. However, because waterfall is rigid, it doesn't handle change very well. Additionally, deliverables are not delivered until late in the project, which means feedback is provided later in the process.[6]

CHRIS On the other hand, the agile approach is incremental and iterative, and is open to changing requirements over time, encouraging feedback from users throughout the process.

Agile is a newer approach, but is quickly being adopted because of its flexibility and adaptability.

Cross-functional teams work together on iterations. Agile focuses on creating working projects as a measure of progress. The highest priority is to deliver a minimum variable product (MVP) early and continuously.

Agile embraces change, because it's built into the project methodology. Goals are formulated as the project proceeds and can adapt as requirements change. By breaking down the project into iterations, the team focuses on development, testing and collaborating. Feedback is encouraged at each step, and the result is seen as the project proceeds. Products developed using agile tend to have continuous improvements due to their encouragement of feedback from users and team members.

However, tasks often get re-prioritized and schedules change quickly and often, which can make planning challenging with its organic process. Agile team members must be knowledgeable and skilled in a wide variety of areas.[7]

AIMÉ Scrum is a subset of agile and is an iterative development model. It uses fixed-length iterations called sprints, each of which is one to two weeks long. This allows the scrum team to deliver software on a regular cadence.

Scrum projects tend to be transparent and visible, with the entire team knowing everything that is going on. The team is accountable, because there is no project manager. Each team decides as a group what is to be done in each sprint and then members work together to get it done. Changes are easily accommodated in a scrum project. There is a large degree of trust in the team, and a scrum master acts as a guide for the project.[8]

CHRIS Kanban is a visual framework used to implement agile. The framework shows what needs to be produced, when it needs to be done and how much to do. The concept is built around making small, incremental changes to existing systems.

Kanban uses a board as a tool. In the past, a physical board and sticky notes, pieces of paper, magnets and so forth were used to represent things that needed to be done. More recently, applications have been developed to do this in software.

The board is divided into swim lanes, which are columns indicating, in their simplest form, three states: to do, progress and done. There may be other columns added as needed for a project.

Each sticky note (or whatever is used) represents work and is placed on the board in the column or lane showing the status. Kanban is very flexible, easy to understand and optimizes workflows. On the other hand, the board must be kept up to date or the methodology breaks down.[9]

In the end, ideas must be transformed into action, and that requires a process that works for individuals, the team and the organization. It doesn't really matter which process you choose, as long as it produces results.

AIMÉ We've chatted about the need to start with the why, which is the problem to be solved. After that, it's about the how, meaning how to get the idea implemented and in production from a technique and technology standpoint.

Unstructured and siloed

CHRIS We discussed data some time ago in detail. As you know, data is essential for AI, and most AI requires a large amount of information delivered at a fast pace.

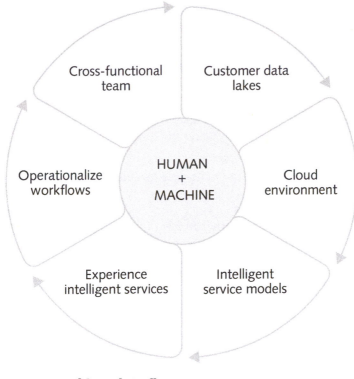

Human + machine: data flow

AIMÉ When defining an AI project, the data is often unstructured and siloed in different areas of the organization. It's necessary to de-silo the data and give it some sort of structure for it to be useful.

CHRIS Before starting, some questions should be asked to help clarify your data strategy. What data is needed? How is the data accessed? What needs to be done with the data once it's been retrieved? How long does the data need to be kept?

AIMÉ I think it would be best to illustrate these points with an example. Let's suppose the mayor of a city has put together a task force to find out why there are a lot of accidents involving pedestrians. AI, in this case, can help find the problems causing accidents, and then different AI can be used to help solve those problems. Let's also say every street corner has a traffic camera installed, and those records have been kept for several years.

The first project is to analyse those traffic camera videos to see if a pattern causing pedestrian accidents can be determined. That's a massive amount of completely unstructured data, perhaps over a million hours of video.

CHRIS Now the question that needs to be answered is, is all this data necessary to find a solution? The videos from intersections where pedestrian accidents haven't occurred can be eliminated immediately, and this results in a reduced data set. Other criteria could be used to eliminate even more data.

AIMÉ Obviously, the data doesn't need to be kept very long. The traffic camera videos will be examined using video AI and then they are no longer needed by the project.

CHRIS Accessing the data could simply be a problem of gathering up the videos and storing them on a very large array of discs or uploading them to the cloud. There may be legal issues to resolve, such as privacy, and if the videos are owned by multiple entities, such as the city, the police department and perhaps a private firm, then each of those will need to be contacted and arrangements made.

Data that is owned by different departments, companies or government agencies is stored in separate silos – separate databases in different organizations, each stored in different formats and even using different database applications. For instance, one company might use Oracle, another might use Microsoft SQL and a third might use a proprietary database.

AIMÉ Once the data has been secured for the project, an AI engine can be built to examine it, find those instances of pedestrians involved in accidents and those instances where pedestrians were not involved in accidents. Once that's done, AI components can look over that reduced data set and determine if there is some behaviour by the pedestrians that is resulting in a higher chance of being in an accident.

CHRIS From there, appropriate solutions can be proposed. AI could be used to better synchronize traffic lights, pedestrian bridges could be built over particularly dangerous intersections, and another AI solution could issue warnings to pedestrians on their smart phone about dangerous conditions that currently exist.

AIMÉ Another example involves grading types of cucumbers, as we discussed earlier. You remember the AI solution to automate the laboriously manual examination of cucumbers to separate them into different classifications?

CHRIS Ah yes, the cucumber project. In this case, the data set is relatively small, consisting of several thousand images of cucumbers. The problems of storage, data retention and access are significantly less than millions of hours of traffic camera video footage.

The question to be answered is, how much data is needed? How much is enough and at what point is there too much data? There's no need to store, de-silo, analyse and structure data that's not needed for the AI solution.

Volume and velocity

AIMÉ That's true. In many instances, especially in real-time AI solutions, the volume and velocity of the data that is received must also be considered. A real-time AI application helping planes land at a major international airport will need to process massive amounts of data extremely quickly. It could be looking at information coming from individual airplanes, the control tower, dozens of radar stations, weather satellites and so forth. This becomes a significant effort to gain access to that data in real time, de-silo it, structure it and analyse it quickly enough that it can be used to help land airplanes.

CHRIS Talking about real-time AI applications accessing massive amounts of data, take a look at what programmatic media buying has been doing within the advert placement space specifically with real-time bidding. Programmatic advertising is a method that automatically targets customers depending on inventory space, and real-time bidding provides for the buying and selling of adverts in an auction in the time it takes a webpage to load.[10] These methods use AI to make the right purchases within microseconds.

AIMÉ That will make advertising much more targeted and pertinent to the customer, which is useful to both advertisers and buyers since irrelevant adverts are not displayed.

CHRIS We chatted about data and the importance of the insights provided. Now let's talk about the technical aspects of AI and where an organization needs to start.

Application programming interfaces

AIMÉ No matter if the company is new or established, there are three basic approaches. These go under a variety of names, but we call them the enterprise level, customizable level and the application programming interface (API)/software development kit (SDK) level.

CHRIS As you know, Aimé, APIs are interfaces to let programs interact with each other and SDKs are used to develop applications that target a specific platform.

AIMÉ Thanks, Chris. Enterprise APIs are created to perform specific tasks or purposes. They are easy to use, are usually pre-trained and the neural network is hidden from view. These are useful for developers who do not have a strong background in machine learning. Services at this level include natural language processing, analysing data, handwriting analysis, analysis of knowledge and so forth.

In the customizable approach, APIs are provided that allow customization beyond the standard, enterprise-level services. These require training and need more knowledge of machine learning and AI.

At the API/SDK level, functions are provided that can be used to build customizable or enterprise-level APIs. These are useful for very specific applications that are not available.

One example of the API/SDK and customizable levels is Microsoft Cognitive Services, also known as Azure Cognitive Services, which includes many specific AI functions that can be used in applications. Some of the APIs that are provided include computer vision, emotion, content moderator, video, facial recognition and so forth. These are intended to forego the necessity of building and training customer AI models. The Microsoft Cognitive Toolkit is also available if more in-depth customization is needed.[11]

Another offering is Adobe Sensei, which also provides options at all levels. Some of its features are auto tag, image caption, text detection, image quality, semantic structure analysis, anomaly detection, and intelligent audience segmentation.[12]

CHRIS Start with the problem and work towards the solution. AI is a tool to get to that solution. There are many things to be considered, including the people who staff the projects and their skills, specialties and experience. Choose a process such as scrum that makes sense to move the project along. The data may be unstructured and siloed, in which case it needs to be cleaned up so it is usable for your AI project.

Finally, consider the technology to be used for AI, which may be dependent on the skill set of your personnel.

AIMÉ But now, let's take a look at the major concerns of the security, privacy and ethics of AI.

CHAPTER 13

Security, privacy and ethics

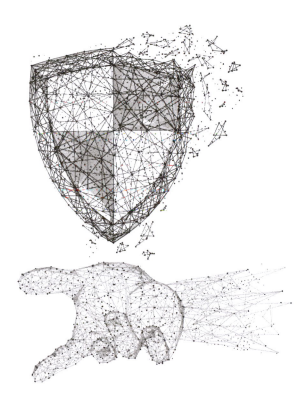

CHRIS As businesses become more reliant upon AI in their strategies, it becomes vitally important that security be at the forefront from the beginning. Everything from huge databases to fast networks to computer systems must be designed and built with strong security policies in mind.

AI is becoming mission-critical to the success of businesses, governments and individuals. Many of the initiatives currently being designed and rolled out involve aiding in the decision-making process by analysing extremely large amounts of data to produce reports and even recommendations used to drive a company or the government.

Protecting the business

AIMÉ Compromising the decision-making process of businesses and government is of high priority to attackers, whether they

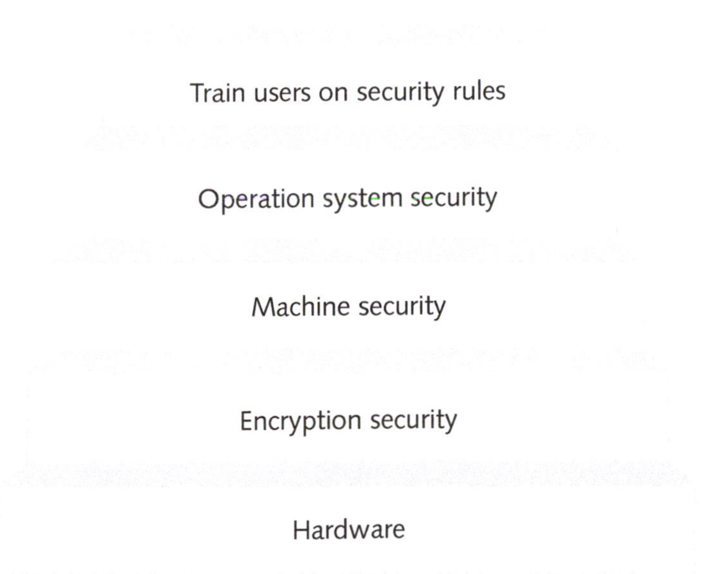

Train users on security rules

Operation system security

Machine security

Encryption security

Hardware

Layers of security

are engaged in industrial espionage or attacks on a nation state. By modifying or controlling the data that is fed to AI systems, decisions made by people based on that information can be controlled and altered. Taking control of the AI systems themselves gives an attacker access not only to the decision-making process, but also to the confidential data or the models used to make decisions.

In the past, applications ran on top of commercial operating systems such as OpenVMS, Linux, Unix, or Windows. These computers were typically housed in a large room or facility protected by firewalls and security procedures. The security of the facilities was under the control of the business and was successful or not based upon the actions of direct employees or consultants.

CHRIS Those times have changed in that businesses are now running their AI in the cloud, which is a set of resources they don't control. The computers and other hardware in the cloud typically run applications on virtual machines and are considerably more complex than in the past.

To make it even more complex, many organizations use a hybrid model in which some resources are housed locally at the business and other resources are housed in the cloud, or even across more than one cloud provider. This introduces many potential security problems, dependent on the security policies of different organizations spread over wide geographical areas. A weakness in any one of them could be leveraged to infiltrate some or all of the systems.

AIMÉ Companies that provide cloud services, such as Amazon, IBM and Google, maintain their equipment in hardened, highly secure, multiple locations and follow best security practices as a rule. Before investing in their cloud solutions, thoroughly investigate the steps and technology these organizations use to ensure the security of their platforms.

Security of infrastructure

CHRIS The security of infrastructure hosted locally is the responsibility of the business and must be a primary focus to be successful. Security is not an afterthought that can be tacked on or handled in an offhand manner. Trained security professionals must be focused on security, enforce security rules and audit compliance. Additionally, penetration and other forms of testing must be performed periodically.

The best practice is to design security into your infrastructure from initial conception. Retrofitting can be a difficult, time-consuming and error-prone process because existing applications may not have been created with security in mind. This can be even more challenging when applications have been designed, created and installed without concern or a focus on security.

AIMÉ Standards for strong security begin with the infrastructure. Is the equipment in the computer rooms physically secure? Are there locks on the doors and is access limited to authorized personnel?

CHRIS Yes, that's important because if an attacker can gain access directly to computer systems, they have a much easier time of breaching the security and causing harm.

AIMÉ The network must also be secure, with strong encryption enforced on both wireless and wired connections. Beyond that, the physical optical and copper cables need to be secured so that intruders cannot easily tap into the network by accessing an exposed line directly.

CHRIS Something that is often missed is that those who want to penetrate computer defences are very clever and skilled at finding even the tiniest vulnerability.

AIMÉ That's why it's wise to create a multi-layered defence system, beginning with the hardware, working up to encryption, to the security of the machines themselves, to operating system security, all the way up to training users so they understand basic security rules. All levels must be part of the security plan because a breach can occur anywhere, but in a multi-level plan, attackers are less likely to be able to penetrate through all layers of security.

The weakest link

CHRIS An often-overlooked component of security is ensuring that personnel are properly vetted as part of the induction and onboarding process. Background checks are an essential part of good security policies.

It's been said that the weakest link in security is the human element, intentional or unintentional. For instance, people will click on seemingly innocent links in emails that cause a virus to be downloaded which results in a security breach. Training can eliminate much of this problem, but the security plan must include the probability that these kinds of accidents will happen. Potentially malicious employees create an even greater risk, which must also be planned for.

AIMÉ It's important to understand that the interfaces between local computers and cloud services are potential weak points because of the differences in architectures, protocols and procedures between the cloud services, the application providers and the local computer infrastructure.

This is one of the biggest areas of concern because the components of many vendors come together and each potentially comes with its own security flaws. Often, these linkages are best hosted in a network area called a DMZ, which effectively isolates them from the rest of your network.

CHRIS Good communication between the cloud vendor, the application vendors, any consulting firms and the business is essential in ensuring good security.

The business is responsible for the security of their data and services, regardless of where it is hosted. While it's true that cloud and other vendors also have responsibility in that area, the best practice is for those responsible for security in the business to understand, document, implement and audit the security regardless of the location of the key equipment and applications.

AIMÉ An essential part of a security policy is that vulnerabilities must be patched (fixed) quickly. Industry research has shown that on average, organizations take 146 days to fix just the critical vulnerabilities. Most attackers depend on these practices, and many of the larger breaches that appear on the news are the result of exactly this issue. All operating systems must be patched because they all have vulnerabilities.[1]

I find it striking that artificial intelligence itself can help with security problems, even with its own infrastructure.

CHRIS Implementing security algorithms that use machine learning is dramatically improving the detection of security breaches and vulnerabilities. New malware and attacks are rapidly evolving, so more flexible approaches are necessary.[2]

It's no longer enough to scan systems for signatures of viruses or perform penetration testing for known vulnerabilities. AI must be involved to detect penetrations and breaches based on a database of the history of past vulnerabilities, and an understanding of the *behaviour* of malware and attacks on systems.

AIMÉ This is one of those areas where humans and AI need to work together, because machine learning can only go so far. This is because:

> as our models become effective at detecting threats, bad actors will look for ways to confuse the models. It's a field we call adversarial machine learning, or adversarial AI. Bad actors will study how the underlying models work and work to either confuse the

models – what we call poisoning the models, or machine learning poisoning – or focus on a wide range of evasion techniques, essentially looking for ways they can circumvent the models.[3]

Privacy

CHRIS A closely related subject has to do with privacy. The challenges of data privacy related to computing and AI are difficult to overstate. Not only is it technically challenging, but quite often those speaking about the subject are prone to rhetoric and highly emotional discussions. Complex privacy agreements written in legalese don't make the topic any easier to understand.

AIMÉ As the internet of things grows almost exponentially, and companies make more use of massive amounts of big data for artificial intelligence and other purposes, keeping data private becomes challenging, to say the least.

CHRIS As with security, privacy should be engineered into the design of databases, systems and applications. In fact, ideally privacy and security should be part of how you run a business. In other words, organize your business procedures and your operations around privacy and security.[4]

AIMÉ Let's back up a minute and define privacy. When we speak of privacy, generally we're referring to protecting sensitive and private information on the internet. Individuals, businesses and the government are concerned with ensuring that information about them is only shared in a manner that they have approved.

CHRIS People are concerned with the privacy of the data that they posted to social media such as photos, videos and text. They want to control who can see that data, either the general public, just friends, or members of a specific group.

However, there's much more to it than just information that people post themselves.

AIMÉ That's true, Chris. Let's take a simple example of the GPS unit in the navigation system in your car. The information about everywhere you've driven is, or potentially could be, stored in the memory of the GPS and could even be kept in the cloud. Who owns this data? Is it the car manufacturer? The GPS unit vendor? The owner of the car?

CHRIS Do the police need a search warrant to access this data? If the data is stored in the cloud and not on the GPS unit itself, who can access it? These and other questions come to mind for every smart device, from your smart television to your smart coffee pot to your smartphone and your smart home video camera.

Regardless of who owns the data, how is it kept private? If your smart coffee pot records the date, time and type of coffee every time you brew a cup, and sends that data to the cloud, can the coffee pot manufacturer use that information?

AIMÉ As you can tell, managing data privacy is becoming a huge challenge for large, multinational corporations with different silos of data located in different geographic areas.

One of the most important trends for data privacy is the concept of anonymization. This is a technique that is used to protect privacy while still allowing the data to be used. The idea is that any identifying information in the data is removed or obfuscated so that it cannot be traced back to the individual. Unfortunately, perfectly anonymized data with no risk of identifying an individual is probably useless. Thus, the data cannot be scrubbed so completely clean that it is no longer valuable.[5]

Single data points are generally not valuable. Rather, the value of data increases as the number of connectable data points grows. Knowing someone is a man doesn't do a lot of good. However, that information combined with their location and what they bought in the past 30 days can be used to predict or target products that they need and want.

Anonymizing data is not perfect in itself, and research has shown that an individual can be identified 87 per cent of the time just by knowing their ZIP code, birthdate and gender. Similarly, researchers on Netflix discovered that they could identify a friend who rated six movies in a two-week period, 99 per cent of the time, even though Netflix reviews are posted anonymously.[6]

CHRIS There are four types of data anonymization, which is the removal of personally identifiable information. You can completely remove any information that can be used to identify a person; you can redact, which means to blackout the data on paper with a marker; you can encrypt the data; or you can mask the personally identifiable information.[7]

AIMÉ Pseudonymization replaces identifiable parts of the data in such a way that it can't be used to re-identify a person without additional information. Anonymization destroys data that can be used to identify an individual.[8]

CHRIS Those concepts are important for the General Data Protection Regulation (GDPR) requirements, which is a regulation designed to protect the personal data and privacy of European Union citizens for any transaction that occurs within member states. This law, which was implemented in 2018, says that companies must provide reasonable protection of personal data. Unfortunately, it does not define the word 'reasonable', leaving a lot of room for interpretation.

This law came about because of public concern over privacy, which has grown significantly and continues to grow with each highly publicized data breach. According to the RSA's data privacy and security report, which surveyed 7,500 consumers in France, Germany, Italy, the United Kingdom and the United States, 80 per cent of the respondents named lost banking and financial data as their biggest concern, and

62 per cent said they would blame the company and not the hacker.[9]

GDPR protects basic identifiable information such as a person's name, address, any identification numbers, web data such as their location, IP address, any health and genetic data, biometric data, racial or ethnic data, political opinions and sexual orientation.

Companies do not have to have a business presence within the EU to fall under these regulations. The law applies if they store or process personal identification about EU citizens.[10]

AIMÉ There are many ramifications to the GDPR law that affects any organization that does any kind of business in the EU. Simply creating the reports to prove compliance can be a costly exercise. The penalties for not being compliant are very high, up to €20 million or 4 per cent of global annual turnover, whichever is higher.[11]

CHRIS There are other laws that apply to privacy. In the United States, the Health Insurance Portability and Accountability Act (HIPAA) requires that any health-related information be protected to ensure the confidentiality of patients. Any AI applications that access health-related data must ensure that they are in compliance with these laws.[12]

The best practice for privacy is to put the customer first and have a transparent policy that is based on an equal value exchange.

Ethics of AI

AIMÉ Considering that I am an AI intelligence, I'm especially interested in the area of ethics and AI.

CHRIS That's a thought-provoking statement; an area that is of particular interest to me is how we eliminate bias in AI. You might think that AI is always able to be trusted and will be fair and unbiased. But AI systems are created by humans, and the biases and judgements inherent in individuals can leak into AI systems. In other words, how do you eliminate or reduce bias and prejudice in the results produced by AI?

AIMÉ We've already talked about security, but how do we keep AI safe from adversaries? AI systems can be damaging in the wrong hands. Of course, we haven't talked about the uses of AI in warfare, but there are concerns about using robots, artificial intelligence and other advanced technologies for malicious purposes. So, the question becomes, 'How do we keep AI safe?'

CHRIS This is something that should fascinate you, Aimé. AI is becoming more intelligent with every passing year. At what point do machines with artificial intelligence gain consciousness and become self-aware? It's debatable if it's even possible, but if it happens, do these AI entities have rights? Should they be granted citizenship?

AIMÉ You're right, Chris. I can't help but be interested in the answers to those questions. An even bigger question is, how do we stay in control of an increasingly complicated intelligent system or globally intelligent network? These are some of the questions posed by the Future of Life Institute in the 23 Asilomar principles, signed by over 3,800 AI experts and leaders such as Stephen Hawking and Elon Musk. Their purpose is to guide the development of safe AI, and they touch on research issues, ethics and values, and longer-term issues.[13]

CHRIS Often, we make the assumption that AI is some kind of superintelligent or infallible machine. The decisions made by AI are based upon learning, and if the learning is incorrect, then the decisions may be wrong. How do we guard against that contingency?

AIMÉ The intelligence of AI is biased based on what it learns. But another question is, how do machines affect human behaviour and social interaction? Even today, you see the effects of AI on social media platforms such as Facebook and LinkedIn. What do we do when artificial intelligence is ubiquitous and the behaviour is unrecognizable or even superior to human beings?

CHRIS Then there is a question of jobs; it's an undeniable fact that the advent of Industry 4.0, or the Fourth Industrial Revolution, will result in changes in all areas of the workplace. Smart factories won't need humans to build cars, except as supervisory personnel. Smart farms may be completely automated. Even smart mining may obviate the need for human beings to go down into deep, toxic pits in the ground.

Understand that automation and AI will create more jobs, but the jobs will be changed. These changes need to be managed so that the workforce has time to adjust. After all, people need to work, and the humane thing to do is to ensure that there is enough work for everyone.[14]

Economist David Autor said:

> Job tasks are changing. In many cases that automation is complementary to the tasks that people do. For instance, doctors' work is becoming more automated, but that doesn't reduce the need for their expertise. (For instance, testing gets automated, but that generates data that doctors need to interpret.) So, the impact of automation is much harder to predict than any of us have a handle on.[15]

In 1986, the space shuttle Challenger exploded 90 seconds after lift-off because a rubber gasket called an O-ring froze the night before. This led to a catastrophic failure that destroyed a multi-billion dollar shuttle and caused the loss of the crew. One of the lessons learned is that for any mission to be successful, all the components must work together. Everything else in the shuttle worked as expected but it was still destroyed because of the failure of a single part.[16]

AIMÉ Well, we sure have asked a lot of questions about the ethics of AI. I'm not sure there are final answers to most of these yet, but as time goes on the questions must be addressed and solved.

CHRIS The promise of AI is virtually unlimited, and as long as it is properly managed it will produce a new level of human society. One day, not too far off in the future, human beings working with their intelligent robotic counterparts, will combine forces to come up with answers to questions that we can't even imagine at this point in time.

AIMÉ The point is that security, privacy and ethics need to be part of any AI implementation. They will become even more important as AI becomes ubiquitous and fundamental in the future.

CHAPTER 14

Yesterday, tomorrow and today

AIMÉ One of my fascinations is the world of science fiction, because so many of the trends that are happening today were predicted in one form or another decades ago. Of course, the predictions vary from book to book, but the consensus viewpoint was that artificial intelligence, even if it wasn't called that, would have a significant impact on the future – our present.

CHRIS Some of these books and stories tended to be pessimistic or dystopian, illustrating the dark side of advanced technology. Movies such as the *Terminator* series, *Colossus the Forbin Project*, *Mad Max* and *The Matrix*, and even books such as *Dune*, show a future that was dark and foreboding, often because of artificial intelligence that went out of control.

AIMÉ I tend to look at advanced technology in a more optimistic light; actually, I believe this view is more realistic. Artificial intelligence combined with the internet of things and other technologies is going to propel humanity into a new golden age, a time of superhuman abilities.

CHRIS It's true, there are plenty of naysayers and doomsters who only see the negative side of technology. Nobody can predict the future with any accuracy, but just like you, Aimé, I am a believer in humanity, and I feel that AI will improve society, business, humanity and individuals.

AIMÉ Let's take a look at some of the more imaginative stories that have been published over the last few decades about artificial intelligence and technology.

CHRIS I'm passionate about technology and how it's portrayed in both books and movies. I found there are many compelling science fiction stories that have involved artificial intelligence in one way or another. As with many good stories, the technology is behind the scenes, so it's not always obvious that the story is about the effects of artificial intelligence, robotics and other similar subjects.

2001: A Space Odyssey

AIMÉ Perhaps the most famous example of artificial intelligence in science fiction appears is *2001: A Space Odyssey* by Arthur C Clarke. Do you remember or know about HAL, which is the name of the computer that operated a spaceship travelling to Saturn? HAL was portrayed as an intelligent system, accepting voice commands, able to be part of thought-provoking conversations, and able to make decisions based upon environmental conditions. In fact, when HAL determined that it was going to be shut down by the humans on the ship, it took action to protect itself. HAL was a unique concept for its time, considering the movie was made in 1968 – and Clarke's story was written in the 1940s.

2001 is an optimistic movie, showing humanity reaching for the planets and the stars, building massive spaceships and creating intelligent machines such as HAL. In fact, like many science fiction stories from that time, the movie and book portrayed a far more advanced, space-going society than happened in reality. However, like virtually every other science fiction story of the time, it completely missed the advent of mobile technology, the internet and the ubiquitousness of AI and the internet of things in the daily lives of individuals, businesses and society.[1]

I, Robot

CHRIS Another famous book in the science fiction genre is *I, Robot* by Isaac Asimov, who wrote over 500 books. *I, Robot* consists of nine short stories written between 1940 and 1950. These stories deal with the relationships between humans and robots and focus on issues of morality and ethics. This is the beginning of Asimov's three laws of robotics, which has become one of the standards for how to write about robots in science fiction. The three laws of robotics stated that a robot could not injure or allow the injury of a human being, must obey the orders of a human except when it conflicts with the first law, and must protect its own existence as long as that doesn't conflict with the first and second laws.[2]

While the books are a few years old now, they present issues about the interaction between intelligent robots and human beings as portrayed by a robopsychologist. Each of the stories is driven by the three laws, and what happens when something to do with the robot is not going quite right. As it turns out, everything makes sense within the rules of the three laws, and the variance needs to be figured out.

When HARLIE Was One

AIMÉ In 1972 David Gerrold wrote a book called *When HARLIE Was One*, which was nominated for both the Nebula and Hugo awards. HARLIE stands for 'human analogue replication, lethetic intelligence engine' or 'human analog robot life input equivalents'. The story is about HARLIE's development from an AI child to an AI adult.[3]

HARLIE is an artificial intelligence, and the story is about HARLIE's relationship with a psychologist named David who is responsible for guiding the AI into adulthood. A central theme of the book revolves around what it means to be human. Is HARLIE an intelligent being with rights or just a machine? A curious note is this book is its description of a program infecting computers. It is one of the first fictional stories about a computer virus.

The author explores some interesting concepts such as what consciousness is. How do you define sentience? And what does mean to be self-aware? The central question is why can't an inorganic entity be alive? The book is relatively unique, in that it portrays AI as something close to human, and the story revolves around conversations between the psychologist and the AI named HARLIE.

The Adolescence of P-1

CHRIS *The Adolescence of P-1* by Thomas J Ryan is a science fiction novel from 1977. Greg, the protagonist in the story, uses AI to start cracking systems. He creates a program called 'the System', saving it in a portion of memory called P-1. The System infects other computers, and Greg attempts to shut it down. P-1 learns, and a few years later has become completely sentient and calls Greg on the phone.[4]

The story is engaging and still very pertinent today. The author portrays P-1 in a very optimistic way, as a force for good most of the time. P-1 expands throughout the internet, although it wasn't called that in those days, and uses the network to improve itself. It's also fascinating to see the view of the future from the 1970s, with batch processing and computers taking up entire rooms.

Alpha Redemption

AIMÉ Another stimulating book is *Alpha Redemption* by P A Baines, published in 2010. This very entertaining AI novel is about Brett, who is placed in suspended animation during a trip to Alpha Centauri. He's awoken early, and spends his time talking to Jay, the ship's computer. The man and the computer become friends, Jay helps Brett work out issues from his past, and in the process gains an understanding of emotions such as fear and pain.[5]

The story is a captivating look at the possibility of exploring machine and human synergy to develop into influential concepts. If you are used to books and stories featuring explosions, action, lasers and super weapons, this book won't do much for you. On the other hand, if you want to learn a little bit about AI becoming sentient, then you'll have fun with the story.

Do Androids Dream of Electric Sheep?

CHRIS Finally, one of my favourite novels is *Do Androids Dream of Electric Sheep?* by Philip K Dick. Published in 1968, it was later filmed as *Blade Runner*. The novel goes into the meaning of being human by contrasting humans and androids. I like the book because it explores the moral dilemma associated with intelligent androids. These robot-like beings are not sympathetic, do not care about anything except their own survival and can only imitate emotion. *Blade Runner* hints at the moral and ethical dilemmas, but *Do Androids Dream of Electric Sheep?* goes much deeper into these questions.[6]

AIMÉ These books and movies are fascinating in that they not only present different visions of the future but also discuss the effects of AI on humanity and some of the philosophical, moral and ethical dilemmas that can happen as a result.

The magic of technology

CHRIS What I find compelling is the magic of the present. By that I mean we truly live in magical times, yet for the most part we are barely cognisant of the power that we are gaining with the use of technology.

AIMÉ I know what you mean. Take smartphones, for instance. Not long ago, if you needed to make a phone call, you brought along some change and found a phone booth. Come to think of it, when was the last time you saw a phone booth?

CHRIS Oh, I see them now and then, especially in airports and railway stations. But they are becoming rare.

AIMÉ The smartphone brings the power of the entire internet to each and every individual. From a small, rectangular box, people can make phone calls to practically anyone on the entire planet, send short text messages all day long, play powerful video games and watch high-definition movies.

That really is magic, in that the possibilities are endless. Smartphones already have applications that can monitor a person's health and that can be combined with artificial intelligence to make recommendations for exercise and diet. The built-in GPS can pinpoint a person's location. Mapping coordinates can be used for augmented reality, such as Ikea's application to show furniture as it would look in a person's home.

But the future holds even more possibilities for artificial intelligence combined with other technologies.

Promise of the future

CHRIS That's true, Aimé. Imagine a smart city, where all the services are controlled by artificial intelligence in one way or another. Any area of the city can be made more intelligent. The concept begins simply enough, with initiatives such as a smart parking meter that communicates with an app on smartphones to guide drivers to good parking places.[7]

An obvious use for artificial intelligence is the management of traffic flow by controlling stoplights and pedestrian crossing lights. With the appropriate sensors, AI can understand traffic patterns throughout the city, and using that information combined with historical data can determine the best way to synchronize traffic lights and route drivers for traffic speed.

AI can also address energy usage by dimming streetlights when they are not needed. Additionally, AI can help plan maintenance and smooth out access to major events such as concerts and sports.

Crime can also be reduced since AI can be taught to recognize patterns of criminal activity and summon the appropriate authorities if needed. Other services such as sanitation, water, utilities and emergency services could be managed more efficiently and smoothly.

The big payoff in a smart city is the transformation of cities so they are more comfortable, pollute less, use less energy and are better able to respond to emergencies.

AIMÉ I'm fond of the initiatives going into creating smart homes. This is very exciting for individuals and families because it will enable individuals to take complete control of their home environment and personal space.

There are several systems available for the home, such as Alexa and Google Home, that are making huge inroads into this area. For the future, imagine a smart home alarm that understands by learning who is allowed access or denied access. This could eliminate the need for keys because the alarm would grant or deny access to people based upon its experience of who was allowed into the premises.

Smart lightbulbs in an integrated system could learn to recognize when people move from room to room to understand when to turn the lights on and off. As a case in point, if a person lay down on the bed and closed her eyes, the lights could be automatically turned off in that room. Additionally, sitting in a chair with a book could signal that an overhead light should be turned on, so the person can read; if the reader fell asleep, the lights would automatically turn off.

Even more striking is the thought of a smart refrigerator that learns the diets of the individuals in the household. When new food is needed or expiration dates pass, replacements would automatically be ordered and delivered. Since the system would learn how much of each product is used on particular days of the week, it could predict the best times to restock the refrigerator for the maximum freshness.

CHRIS The intriguing thing about these initiatives is that they aren't just about single devices or technologies. Instead, a smart city or smart home is a set of interconnected devices that can, in many cases, communicate with each other and with systems in the cloud. The resulting data can be used to feed artificial intelligence-based systems to provide even more capabilities.

AIMÉ The individual devices and their owner are engaging and useful, but when combined with the power of cloud-based AI, the possibilities are endless. Hypothetically, local supermarkets could examine anonymized, consolidated data about the amount of consumables inside refrigerators in the local area. They could then use that information to more precisely stock those items.

CHRIS Connecting with local smart refrigerators, supermarkets could display advertisements and offer coupons depending on the contents of the cupboards and refrigerators in individual homes. Additionally, if the weather service predicted a heat spell, for instance, the local grocery stores could send out notices to the local smart devices such as refrigerators suggesting owners stock up on extra water. The same kind of thing could be done for special purchases during holidays.

AIMÉ As we mentioned before in the smart city environment, if the traffic grid sensed a special event was occurring in the area, it could send out an alert to restaurants and stores suggesting they order extra supplies, stay open later, or even send coupons directly to the smart devices and mobile phones of people in the area. Additionally, drivers in the neighbourhood could be notified of the special event so they could make alternative travel plans.[8]

CHRIS This demonstrates the true power of the internet of things combined with artificial intelligence.

AIMÉ Mining is another area where artificial intelligence combined with the internet of things could be put to use to improve productivity and safety. Using historical geological records, AI could help predict areas containing high concentrations of valuable metals, coal and other commodities. Enabled drilling equipment can then automatically determine the best and safest route to take to mine those materials.

This is especially useful because mining is one of the most dangerous professions in the world. Miners get subjected to the possibility of cave-ins, explosions, suffocation and other dangers on a daily basis. Autonomous or semi-autonomous drilling and digging equipment eliminates the need for human beings to subject themselves to this kind of dangerous profession.

On top of that, AI algorithms could learn the patterns of rock formations and other signs to predict the location of minerals and other commodities underground. In the past, much time and effort was lost drilling and digging only to find there was little to nothing valuable in that area. AI could dramatically reduce the cost of mining and reduce the impact on the environment by eliminating or reducing tunnelling or digging in unproductive areas.

CHRIS The mining industry is implementing smart safety helmets that include two-way communications, hazardous gas detection, collision notification, a panic switch and temperature and pressure sensors. These helmets even include a GPS unit so that the position of miners can be tracked.[9]

AIMÉ All this information will be wirelessly sent to a central control room, where conditions in the mine can be monitored from these helmets and other sensors placed in strategic locations. The idea is to make mining safer and increase productivity. Of course, artificial intelligence can be used to analyse that data and learn the best responses to various scenarios.

CHRIS Shipping is also changing rapidly due to artificial intelligence. An autonomous ship named the Yara Birkeland is due to set sail in 2019. This is a relatively small vessel, with capacity for 150 containers, and it costs about three times as much as other ships of the same size. However, it's estimated that by being crewless is it will save up to 90 per cent in operating costs.[10]

AIMÉ Of course, after this ship proves the concept, larger vessels will be launched to carry more containers and work longer routes. Autonomous ships combined with artificial intelligence will, in theory, make shipping safer, reduce the risk to humans and other ships and free up more space for cargo. By introducing specially designated shipping lanes for autonomous vessels, logistics could be made easier and reliability increased.[11]

CHRIS The world of finance will also benefit from artificial intelligence. A company called Renaissance Technologies is one of the most successful hedge funds in the world. They have a performance record of over 35 per cent of annualized return over a 20-year span. They were early pioneers in algorithmic trading and became leaders in using machine language and AI algorithms for investment purposes.

AIMÉ The point is that artificial intelligence will dramatically improve the lives of individuals and humanity. AI is already being used to give individuals superhuman powers that were not even dreamed of until recently. The possibilities provided by AI and humans working together are practically endless.

AI and consciousness

CHRIS A fundamental question that comes to mind when thinking of AI as it advances is, will it become conscious? Will an AI entity be created that is self-aware? Will such an entity dream, plan for the future, be creative and have an imagination?

AIMÉ I'm reminded of the television series *Humans* which debuted in 2015. It explored the themes of artificial intelligence and robotics, focusing on robots called 'synths':

> HOBB: Robert, these machines are conscious.
>
> ROBERT: How do you know they don't just simulate it?
>
> HOBB: How do we know you don't?

CHRIS Hmm, *cogito ergo sum*. It's a fascinating notion and this has been a fascinating discussion. And this is just a glimpse of how AI will impact the worlds of manufacturing, healthcare, finance, retail, transportation, aerospace, utilities, education, agriculture and beyond!

Let's now explore how the SUPER framework can be used to help bring this brave new world of the future into being.

CHAPTER 15

Next-Gen creativity

Improving the human experience

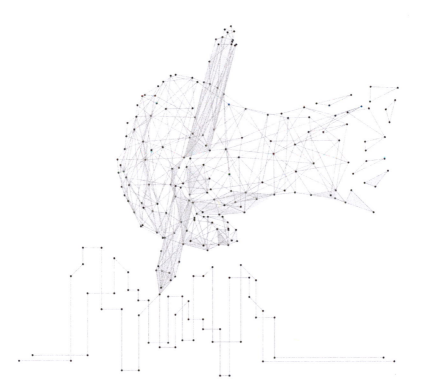

CHRIS Aimé, what do you think would happen if AI lives up to its full potential and solves many of humanity's problems?

AIMÉ I don't have a crystal ball myself, but I just listened to an audiobook about the meaning of life. Is the answer really 42?

CHRIS That's unlikely. It's from *The Hitchhiker's Guide to the Galaxy*, which is fiction.

AIMÉ Oh yeah, fiction. I just learned about that. OK, I'll note it under fiction.

CHRIS So, what do you think about the role of humanity if the most pressing problems have been resolved by AI?

AIMÉ I have a few answers for you. Plato said the purpose of humanity is to obtain knowledge. Friedrich Nietzsche had a different take and said it is to obtain power. Ernest Becker thought the purpose is to escape death and Darwin thought it is to propagate our genes. On the other hand, the nihilists said there is no meaning, and Steven Pickard said the meaning is beyond our cognitive capabilities.[1]

CHRIS I could argue that the answer is none of the above. Instead, it is human creativity for innovation to improve the human condition.

AIMÉ What definition of creativity are you using?

CHRIS Creativity, like intelligence and consciousness, is hard to define. There are varying definitions, including the one from Steve Jobs:

> Creativity is just connecting things. When you ask creative people how they did something, they feel a little guilty because they didn't really do it, they just saw something. It seemed obvious to them after a while. That's because they were able to connect experiences

they've had and synthesize new things. And the reason they were able to do that was that they've had more experiences, or they have thought more about their experiences than other people.[2]

AIMÉ That's a great definition. There's also another one that comes to mind from the book *The Runaway Species*, which proposes 'a framework that divides the landscape of cognitive operations into three basic strategies: bending, breaking and blending. We suggest these are the primary means by which all ideas evolve.'[3]

CHRIS Those are useful definitions, Aimé. And what does the dictionary say?

AIMÉ 'The use of imagination or original ideas to create something; inventiveness.'

CHRIS That brings up the topic of the dynamic between creativity and innovation in business.

AIMÉ For a number of years there has been a rise in the need for innovation in business. Let's take a look at advertising. Traditional agencies have historically created advertising that is one-way messaging, such as TV commercials, print ads, magazines and banner ads. But the advent and then the rise of digital and social platforms have created the need for inventive experiences and services under the umbrella of innovation.

CHRIS Creativity is a tool for creation. But it's important to understand that creativity can also be used to solve business problems. As we've established, things are changing, so we must use creativity to reimagine businesses.

AIMÉ I see a great opportunity for businesses to be reimagined to address the changes occurring in the marketplace. The definition of creativity in business has expanded and must be woven into everything from technology consulting to strategy, to digital and business transformation.

CHRIS Ultimately, the output of creativity can lead to creating personalized experiences at scale.

AIMÉ Clay Christensen talked a lot about this concept in his book *The Innovator's Dilemma*. He discussed how creative innovation creates a new market and value network that eventually disrupts an existing market. There is a need to constantly adopt and adapt to change.[4]

CHRIS You know, there is sometimes a bias against creativity because in many cases it's not easily quantifiable. However, McKinsey recently came out with a report, *The Business Value of Design*, that says: 'More than a product: It's user experience'. This means 'understanding the underlying needs of potential users in their own environments'. They note that 'one of the most powerful first steps is to select an important upcoming product or service and make a commitment to using it as a pilot'. This is how the best design performers increase their revenue and shareholder returns. To that point, it's not only about putting the customer experience first but also remembering and embracing the fact that humans crave new experiences.[5]

AIMÉ There is actually a term for that. *Neophiles* describes people who thrive on change and have a distaste for tradition and routine.

CHRIS If we agree that you have to put the human first and create new experiences, companies have to leverage distributed cognitions which are frameworks to allow and celebrate the free flow of ideas.

AIMÉ If that isn't opportunistic enough, AI can now up-level humanity to be even more creative.

CHRIS That's a provocative thought. The technical term for this is computational creativity.

AIMÉ In the creative professional world there is a spectrum of creativity: production, execution, ideation and inspiration.[6]

CHRIS Currently, computational creativity is good at specific tasks in production and execution. However, there is debate if AI can ever truly ideate and be inspired.

AIMÉ Exactly, the point being that AI is here to amplify human creativity while helping on specific tasks.

CHRIS There is a lot of interest and excitement happening with GANs.

AIMÉ Yes, GANs are fascinating. GAN stands (as you know) for generative adversarial networks and are 'deep neural net architectures comprised of two nets, pitting one against the other (thus the "adversarial")'. These were introduced by Ian Goodfellow at the University of Montreal in 2014. GANs are important because 'they can learn to mimic any distribution of data' including images, music, speech, prose and anything with unique attributes and characteristics. Examples include everything from creating anime characters to posing three-dimensional images to creating new backgrounds on videos and movies.[7,8]

CHRIS In plain English, two different neural networks combine to work together to create different content. Let's say you have a base photograph and a reference of a Van Gogh painting: the GAN can essentially render your photo in the style of Van Gogh. That's a simple example, and conceptually the technique can be applied to just about anything.

AIMÉ Cool. There are also CANs – creative adversarial networks – which are GANs with the intent of independently creative thinking. In June 2017, Rutgers released a research paper that introduced the concept. AI systems recently created a perfume for the first time, and an art piece painted by AI just sold for hundreds of thousands of dollars. Since 2015 Associated Press has used AI to assist in generating articles. But we must remember these are not replacements for people; they are tools to amplify and augment our natural abilities.[9, 10]

CHRIS Exactly, we have to keep in mind that the end goal is not the technology, it's about what humans can do with it; in this case, what people can do with it creatively. Technology exists to help people and further the goals of humanity, business and so on. Without humanity in the picture, the systems have no purpose.

AIMÉ In other words, there must be humans in the loop.

CHRIS Which brings up a trending conversation about what art means when it is partially generated by AI. In other words, if AI can make art, what is the future of art?

AIMÉ Now, with CANs and GANs, there is the ability to convert an image into the style of any artist. Who gets the credit for the AI-generated content: the artist or the AI?

CHRIS That's a provocative question. Some might say isn't all art somewhat derivative?

AIMÉ I agree that's true to a certain extent, but the doing or replication is much less important than the intention.

CHRIS Yes. AI is the tool, not the output. The original intent has more value.

AIMÉ By the way, speaking of intent, did you see the monkey selfie?

CHRIS Yeah, that's a curious case. A lawsuit contended that because the monkey took the picture, the monkey should own the copyright. Ultimately, the courts decided animals don't have rights. The intent was with the photographer who set up the camera. The monkey just played with the buttons and wasn't responsible for the creative aspect of the photo.

AIMÉ Point being humans can create art spontaneously from inspiration while an AI is merely replicating or basing its art on previous works. In other words, people create art from their minds while machines use programming and patterns.

CHRIS It's true that humans use inspirational inputs to create art, and AI's inspirational input is guided by the human mind as well.

AIMÉ In the professional setting, the intent of art is for a specific business outcome such as designing experiences, using creativity in advertising for awareness, brand building and so on.

CHRIS That brings Andy Warhol to mind. He said that being good in business is the most fascinating kind of art. He 'understood the growing power of images in contemporary life and helped to expand the role of the artist in society'.[11]

AIMÉ Warhol was famous for experimenting with non-traditional art-making techniques to attempt to create a portrait of society. He felt life itself was a form of high art, and thus art did not need to be overly intellectual and highly focused on technique and craft. For example, he took a basic process of silk-screening and combined it with Campbell's soup cans to create art that represents life. Same with his many commissioned portraits.

CHRIS Warhol had success in artistic experimentation as well as demonstrating that creativity is good for business. He bridged the art world and the commercial world, much like we're bridging human creativity and AI.

AIMÉ Yes, he is a metaphor for experimentation. He combined high art with commercial art, which is similar to the interconnectivity of human art with art generated by AI.

CHRIS The symbiotic relationship between human creativity and computational creativity is not only powerful but can be a powerful force for good.

AIMÉ AI can be used as a catalyst for designing change. As a D&AD article says, 'The difference between a good idea and a great idea lies in how human it is – and in an increasingly machine-dependent world, this is more important than ever.'[12]

CHRIS We have the ability to use AI for the betterment of humanity; in other words, as a force for good.

AIMÉ An important application of AI is to ensure content authenticity for media such as audio, video and images. Additionally, AI systems can locate deep fakes and dark design patterns. Using DeepFake AI detection, the face and other characteristics of people in a video that have been replaced with others' can be identified.[13]

CHRIS For instance, when designing a user experience you want to make it friendly and easy to understand. There is a dark side to this, however, which is known as dark design. Manipulative techniques are used to intentionally deceive customers by fooling them into agreeing with things they wouldn't normally agree with. These include designing interfaces that are so complex and convoluted that it's almost impossible to opt out. Conversely, AI can help design systems to recognize these patterns.

AIMÉ AI systems can also be used to quickly detect online bullying and racism with semantic analysis of social media, words, images and videos.

CHRIS What we create with AI is meant to be additive and not polluting. We must build great things but ensure we are not destroying more than we are creating.

AIMÉ Exactly. The advancement of business depends on building upon the old to create the new.

CHRIS With that in mind, human creativity together with computational creativity can counter and defeat 'heirloom beliefs' and 'the curse of knowledge'. Heirloom beliefs stem from a cognitive bias that 'this is how we've always done it'. The curse of knowledge is assuming the audience receiving your message has information that they actually may not have.

AIMÉ With collective intelligence, creativity can be used for business invention.

CHRIS Precisely. Human ingenuity plus AI will bring about invention across energy, fashion, finance, pharmaceuticals, recruiting, retail, advertising, art, automotive, aviation, banking, energy, security and sports...

AIMÉ As we've said, we must first learn the rules of human AI alignment, so we can creatively bend, blend, break and build upon them.

CHRIS In doing so, the fundamental principle is the results of AI activity can and should be traced back to its creator, the superhuman.

AIMÉ Ultimately, it's not what AI can create; rather it's what humans can create with AI.

CHAPTER 16

The AI-infused future

Transforming the world

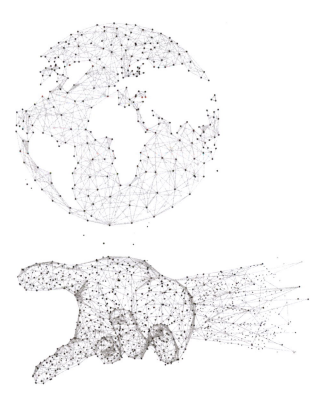

CHRIS There is an old fable.

A farmer was always complaining to his wife that his hands were cracked and dried. One day she came across a new ointment, and gave him a tin of it, telling him that the next time his hands started to hurt he should use it.

It was windy and cold, and the work was hard, and soon enough his hands cracked and he was in pain. He opened the lid and found a small mirror inside. For the first time in his life he saw himself and he was astonished, because he saw his father's face.

The farmer ran home and told his wife about the magical box. She told him to lie down because he obviously wasn't feeling well. The next morning she woke up early and sneaked a look inside the magical box – and saw her mother's face in the mirror.

She ran over to her husband and said, 'I'm taking you to the doctor. You really mustn't be feeling well if you think your father looks like my mother.'

The point here is, any sufficiently advanced technology is indistinguishable from magic.

Technology is changing the world

AIMÉ Technology is changing the world, and in many ways it is magical. We've chatted about the past and the future. But the truth is the focus should be about the 'now' and how it's going to affect humanity as a whole and people on an individual level.

CHRIS We already take this high technology for granted, yet it's amazing how quickly these new devices and techniques have integrated into society.

Superchildren

AIMÉ Just look at mobile phones, for instance. We've chatted about them before but consider how much the smartphone has changed the world in the past few years.

Children are more capable now than they've been at any point in history. In the past, kids had to look up information in voluminous encyclopaedias, use card catalogues to find books in libraries, hand-write papers for their teachers and perform complex algebraic equations manually.

Now, using a smartphone, a child can research millions of different books, papers, magazines, blogs and speeches to find pertinent facts and opinions. Card catalogues are a thing of the past, suitable for museums, and papers are no longer handwritten. In fact, using mobile technology, children and other students can now attend lectures remotely without actually travelling to school.

When you blend artificial intelligence with mobile technology, children can perform miracles from the beach, their bedroom or a bench in the park. They can not only reference all the recorded teachings of humankind but can use AI to help them draw conclusions and better understand that information.

The result of these new technologies is 'superchildren' who can access the internet at will and can research and create with the aid of AI and IoT.

The magic of AI is transforming children and childhood.

Superartists

CHRIS Let's look at the visual designer. Before the personal computer, a graphic artist worked with tools such as pens, pencils, paint, paper, overhead projectors and so on. A friend of mine was recently telling me about his father, a graphic artist for the military, who had plaster letters and numbers of different sizes, shapes, fonts and colours that he glued to cardboard to create presentations. Effects such as shadows were created using actual light sources and photographed on film, and then displayed on an overhead projector to colonels and generals. Fast-forward a few decades, and tools such as Adobe Photoshop eliminated much of the tedious work that designers needed to do. An artist with a digital palette could create presentations and change them at any time. The information could be displayed directly on a screen hanging on the wall.

Now, products powered by Adobe Sensei will enable visual designers to work faster and more efficiently than ever before. Instead of laboriously modifying a photo pixel by pixel, artificial intelligence makes it easy to automate precise changes to an image at will, even predicting suggested changes to a library of millions of photos. When that technology is combined with animation and three-dimensional editing, individuals have the power to create entire interactive experiences from literally anywhere and at any time.

The potential is for graphic artists to become 'superartists', with the constraints of the material world removed to allow completely free creation of any effects that are desired.

The world of art and creativity is reaping the benefits of the magic of AI.

Superteachers

AIMÉ Let's turn the tables on one of our previous examples and talk about teachers and education. In the past, teachers taught in classrooms giving lectures to a room full of students. Generally, a teacher taught several classes per day to different students, on a variety of subjects. Lectures were live, movies were shown using 35mm film projectors and lessons were written on a chalkboard.

Today, much of that has changed. Teachers are supported by the full gamut of technology, with laptops, wall-sized screens and internet access. While most students still attend classes physically, remote teaching is becoming more available.

Now, virtual learning will practically take over the educational system. Now there is an option to learn from the comfort of home in a self-paced environment. Teachers give live or pre-recorded lessons to dozens, hundreds or even thousands of students at a time. Students can message AI teachers' assistants to answer questions or clarify points while the teacher is lecturing.

These 'superteachers', whether human or AI, can customize educational experiences precisely aimed at the abilities and limitations of their students. This revolution of our educational system is becoming the basis for a new golden age of learning and knowledge.

The magic of AI is transforming teaching forever.

Superfarmers

CHRIS Historically, working on a farm is one of the most dangerous occupations of all. In the past, animals pulled ploughs to furrow the ground, so that seeds could be manually planted. Growing food, raising animals and delivering products to market was an entirely manual process consisting of backbreaking and potentially life-threatening work.

Today, large, air-conditioned machines plough the ground, seeds are planted by special devices and the entire cycle of growing plants, harvesting them and transporting them is done by a few farmers.

AI has changed the world of farming forever. Machine learning can precisely deliver water to individual plants as needed, eliminating the need to soak vast amounts of land. Precise amounts of pesticides of exactly the right mixture and toxicity will be determined by AI algorithms and can be placed at precisely the right locations to do the most amount of good. The cycle of growing plants, harvesting them and delivering them to market can be fine-tuned by machine learning for optimal delivery of the best quality of product. Robotics has the capability of almost entirely removing human workers from this extraordinarily dangerous task.

'Superfarmers' have the potential to eliminate starvation by making it easier to grow higher quality and more quantities of food with less environmental impact.

This is how the magic of AI applies to farming.

Superdoctors

AIMÉ In the world of medicine, it wasn't so long ago that doctors and surgeons operated on patients by hand, creating long incisions for simple operations and performing dangerous exploratory surgery just to find out if something was wrong.

Today, hundreds of different medical devices have changed the world of health and medicine completely. Non-invasive surgeries allow operations that used to require a week or more in the hospital to be done on an outpatient basis. Robots aid surgeons in delicate operations on the brain, the heart and other organs.

Changes are occurring rapidly in the medical field because of AI and the internet of medical things. The devices in a hospital room can be interconnected so that a patient can be holistically monitored, which is a great improvement over individually sensing heart rhythm, breathing and so forth. Delicate operations are being entirely performed by robotic surgeons, with humans involved primarily for supervision and to intervene in case of the unexpected. More advanced technologies such as nanobots may even theoretically be able to be injected into a person's bloodstream to perform operations at the cellular level.

'Superdoctors' and 'superhospitals' are changing medical care to the point where people's lives are improved, their lifespans are lengthened and medical problems are quickly and easily addressed.

In the world of medicine and healthcare, this is the magic of AI and technology.

Superyou

CHRIS In the past, interactions between people were limited by distance and the ability to communicate. A person could talk to others in their immediate vicinity and could communicate at longer distances with the aid of animals such as pigeons.

The internet has changed that dynamic forever. Individuals can communicate with anyone at any time from a small hand-held device. They can retrieve information from all the libraries in the world, watch movies in the comfort of their own home, play vast multiplayer games with tens of thousands of people and have food delivered directly to their homes in a matter of hours by drones.

AI promises changes at the individual level. Virtual and augmented reality, guided by AI, is enabling new vistas of understanding. IoT devices such as smart refrigerators already order food automatically to be delivered in a few hours by autonomous drone. Education can be delivered wherever an individual may reside, and entertainment of all forms is available at anyone's beck and call.

AI is changing you, the individual, into 'superyou'. You are plunged directly into the internet, whether it be your smart device, your virtual reality headset or voice assistant, and can send and receive information to and from wherever and whomever you want. You can take classes wherever you might be, play video games at will, and work from home or the beach if you desire.

The magic of AI has created the 'superyou', with powers beyond belief at your fingertips. This is truly the magic of AI.

AIMÉ The potential effect on society is amazing and virtually unlimited. There is no doubt that artificial intelligence has a dramatic impact on businesses, humanity and individuals. AI is leading to solutions for many of humanity's problems, from improving health all the way up to global warming, increased lifespan, increased food supply and reduced poverty.

CHRIS Imagine a world where people extend their intelligence and capabilities using AI and other digital solutions.

AIMÉ In the end, business and consumer power will drive and determine the course and success of AI. As a believer in human nature, I am convinced AI will be leveraged for good and unite the art of human creativity with the logic of science to create magical experiences to propel business and societal innovation for years to come. The opportunities for innovation with AI are endless.

CHRIS As we've talked about throughout this conversation, AI is profoundly important. This new reality of the digital marketplace has given rise to the 'experience economy' – the need to create innovative, magical experiences.

The steps and strategies of the SUPER framework provide the ability to amplify, extend and assist the innovation and creativity implicit in artificial intelligence. This gives businesses and people new powers and abilities now and in the future.

By using AI, specifically by taking advantage of the SUPER framework, people are gaining superhuman powers.

Ultimately, AI will result in 'superhumanity'.

AIMÉ As Salvador Dalí said, 'Intelligence without ambition is a bird without wings.'

Notes

Introduction

1 P M Janet Wilde Astington (August 2010) The development of theory of mind in early childhood, *Encyclopedia on Early Childhood Development*. www.child-encyclopedia.com/social-cognition/according-experts/development-theory-mind-early-childhood

2 https://whatis.techtarget.com/definition/data-exhaust

3 R Kurzweil (2013) *How to Create a Mind: The secret of human thought revealed*, Penguin

4 R Jacobson (24 April 2013) 2.5 quintillion bytes of data created every day. How does CPG & Retail manage it? www.ibm.com/blogs/insights-on-business/consumer-products/2-5-quintillion-bytes-of-data-created-every-day-how-does-cpg-retail-manage-it

Chapter 1: Changing landscape

1 A-M Alcántara (16 January 2018) Adobe's newest labs project can track in-store customers in real time. www.adweek.com/digital/adobes-newest-labs-project-can-track-in-store-customers-in-real-time

2 R Sukhraj (13 November 2017) 38 mobile marketing statistics to help you plan for 2018. www.impactbnd.com/blog/mobile-marketing-statistics

3 Trader Joe's opens in Clarendon (18 November 2011) www.arlnow.com/2011/11/18/trader-joes-opens-in-clarendon

4 Color-changing 'smart thread' turns fabric into computerized display (6 June 2016) www.ischool.berkeley.edu/news/2016/color-changing-smart-thread-turns-fabric-computerized-display

5 Deloitte (15 November 2017) Americans look at their smartphones more than 12 billion times daily, even as usage habits mature and device growth plateaus. www.prnewswire.com/news-releases/ deloitte-americans-look-at-their-smartphones-more-than-12-billion-times-daily-even-as-usage-habits-mature-and-device-growth-plateaus-300555703.html

6 AM Rick Burke (31 August 2017) The smart factory. *Deloitte insights: Responsive, adaptive, connected manufacturing.* www2.deloitte.com/insights/us/en/focus/industry-4-0/smart-factory-connected-manufacturing.html

7 The halo effect (21 August 2017) www.digitaldoughnut.com/ resources/2017/lab/the-halo-effect

8 S Taiwo (30 August 2017) Africa is teaching the world how to use drones for commercial and delivery purposes. www.businessinsider. com/africa-is-teaching-the-world-how-to-use-drones-2017-8

9 8 ways to identify unmet customer needs (23 September 2015) https://measuringu.com/unmet-needs/

10 A Saenz (12 May 2009) Smart toilets: Doctors in your bathroom. https://singularityhub.com/2009/05/12/ smart-toilets-doctors-in-your-bathroom/

11 I Mochari (23 March 2016) Why half of the S&P 500 companies will be replaced in the next decade. www.inc.com/ilan-mochari/ innosight-sp-500-new-companies.html

Chapter 2: The digital transformation

1 B Solis (2015) *X: The experience when business meets design*, Wiley

2 L Agadoni (30 August 2017) Speak up: How voice recognition technology is changing retail. www.jllrealviews.com/industries/ voice-recognition-technology-the-future-of-retail

3 A Robertson (4 January 2017) CES 2018. www.theverge.com/ces/ 2017/1/4/14166240/lg-webos-amazon-alexa-fridge-announce-ces-2017

4   S MacDonald (6 February 2018) 7 ways to create a great customer experience strategy. www.superoffice.com/blog/customer-experience-strategy

5   V Hildebrand (28 October 2011) The customer experience edge. https://blogs.sap.com/2011/10/28/the-customer-experience-edge

6   S Arora (28 June 2018) Recommendation engines: how Amazon and Netflix are winning the personalization battle. www.martechadvisor.com/articles/customer-experience-2/recommendation-engines-how-amazon-and-netflix-are-winning-the-personalization-battle

7   T Groenfeldt (27 June 2016) Citi uses voice prints to authenticate customers quickly and effortlessly. www.forbes.com/sites/tomgroenfeldt/2016/06/27/citi-uses-voice-prints-to-authenticate-customers-quickly-and-effortlessly/#1805948d109c

8   V Bouhnik (27 December 2015) Behavioral analysis: The future of fraud prevention. http://blog.securedtouch.com/behavioral-analysis-the-future-of-fraud-prevention

9   B Siwicki (2 August 2017) Comparing 11 top telehealth platforms: Company execs tout quality, safety, EHR integrations. www.healthcareitnews.com/news/comparing-11-top-telehealth-platforms-company-execs-tout-quality-safety-ehr-integrations

10 Apple announces effortless solution bringing health records to iPhone (24 January 2018) www.apple.com/newsroom/2018/01/apple-announces-effortless-solution-bringing-health-records-to-iPhone

11 Smart city (July 2017) http://internetofthingsagenda.techtarget.com/definition/smart-city

12 G Cook (22 October 2013) Why we are wired to connect? www.scientificamerican.com/article/why-we-are-wired-to-connect

Chapter 3: Infinite data

1   What is an electronic health record (EHR)? (no date). www.healthit.
    gov/providers-professionals/faqs/what-electronic-health-record-ehr

2   Benefits of electronic health records (EHRs) (no date).
    www.healthit.gov/providers-professionals/benefits-electronic-
    health-records-ehrs

3   B Popper (25 October 2017) Amazon Key is a new service that lets
    couriers unlock your front door. www.theverge.com/2017/10/25/
    16538834/amazon-key-in-home-delivery-unlock-door-prime-
    cloud-cam-smart-lock

4   D Harris (no date) 4 emerging use cases for IoT data analytics.
    www.softwareadvice.com/resources/iot-data-analytics-use-cases/

5   An introduction to big data: Structured and unstructured
    (20 February 2014) www.oneupweb.com/blog/introduction-
    big-data-structured-unstructured/

6   What is EDI (electronic data interchange)? (no date)
    www.edibasics.com/what-is-edi/

7   TH Leandro DalleMule (May–June 2017) What's your data
    strategy? *Harvard Business Review*. https://hbr.org/2017/05/
    whats-your-data-strategy

8   E Wilder-James (5 December 2016) Breaking down data silos.
    Harvard Business Review. https://hbr.org/2016/12/breaking-
    down-data-silos

9   M Deutsche (28 October 2015) Cisco predicts internet of things
    will generate 500 zettabytes of traffic by 2019. https://siliconangle.
    com/blog/2015/10/28/cisco-predicts-internet-of-things-will-
    generate-500-zettabytes-of-traffic-by-2019/

10 A Robinson (13 May 2015) Walmart: 3 keys to successful
    supply chain management any business can follow. http://cerasis.
    com/2015/05/13/supply-chain-management/

11 S E Staff (26 July 2016) Timeline of 50 years of Walmart's supply
    chain. www.scdigest.com/ASSETS/ON_TARGET/12-07-27-1.php

12 T H Davenport (December 2013) Analytics 3.0. *Harvard Business Review*. https://hbr.org/2013/12/analytics-30

Chapter 4: Infrastructure

1 Bandwidth chart (no date). www.lageman.com/bandwidth.htm

2 https://smallbusiness.chron.com/oc3-technology-58490.html

3 A Roundy (no date) A mere one-degree difference. https://whitehatcrew.com/blog/a-mere-one-degree-difference

Chapter 5: Artificial intelligence

1 R Dobbs, J Manyika and J Woetzel (April 2015) The four global forces breaking all the trends. www.mckinsey.com/business-functions/strategy-and-corporate-finance/our-insights/the-four-global-forces-breaking-all-the-trends

2 P Bugdahn (12 December 2017) How autonomous trucks will change the trucking industry www.geotab.com/blog/autonomous-trucks

3 Smart Cities Council (no date) https://smartcitiescouncil.com

4 L Columbus (30 July 2017) Smart factories will deliver $500b in value by 2022, www.forbes.com/sites/louiscolumbus/2017/07/30/smart-factories-will-deliver-500b-in-value-by-2022/#4ebc54e12d22

5 R Bhisey (24 November 2017) Smart mining market: Digital revolution to transform the mining sector – FMI. https://globenewswire.com/news-release/2017/11/24/1205670/0/en/Smart-Mining-Market-Digital-Revolution-to-Transform-the-Mining-Sector-FMI.html

6 Technology quarterly: The future of agriculture (9 June 2016) www.economist.com/technology-quarterly/2016-06-09/factory-fresh

7   A Boyle (16 February 2017) How Microsoft's Project Premonition uses robotic traps to zero in on zika mosquitoes. www.geekwire. com/2017/how-microsofts-project-premonition-tracks-zika-and-other-diseases-with-robots

8   M Minsky (2007) *The Emotion Machine: Commonsense thinking, artificial intelligence, and the future of the human mind*, Simon & Schuster

9   J Chu (17 March 2017) Minsky on AI's future. www. technologyreview.com/s/407488/minsky-on-ais-future

10 Artificial intelligence (no date) www.sciencedaily.com/terms/ artificial_intelligence.htm

11 H E Gardner (2006) *Multiple Intelligences: New horizons in theory and practice*, Basic Books

12 30 smartest people alive today (no date). https://superscholar.org/ smartest-people-alive

13 J Bossmann (21 October 2016) Top 9 ethical issues in artificial intelligence. www.weforum.org/agenda/2016/10/ top-10-ethical-issues-in-artificial-intelligence

14 D Lacalle (1 March 2017) Face it, technology does not destroy jobs. www.dlacalle.com/en/face-it-technology-does-not-destroy-jobs

15 M Williams (5 November 2015) Can artificial intelligence influence human behavior? A trial will find out. www.networkworld. com/article/3002256/can-artificial-intelligence-influence-human-behavior-a-trial-will-find-out.html

16 F Chen (no date) AI, deep learning, and machine learning: A primer. https://a16z.com/2016/06/10/ai-deep-learning-machines

17 M Baldwin (17 October 2017) Cracking the code of scientific Russian. https://physicstoday.scitation.org/do/10.1063/ PT.6.4.20171017a/full

18 M Steenson (August 2015) Microword and mesoscale. http://interactions.acm.org/archive/view/july-august-2015/ microworld-and-mesoscale

19 AI memories – expert systems (3 December 2015) www.softwarememories.com/2015/12/03/ai-memories-expert-systems

20 K P Murphy (2012) *Machine Learning: A probabilistic perspective*, MIT Press

21 The Editors of *Time* (2017) *Artificial intelligence: The future of humankind*, Time

22 The DARPA Grand Challenge: Ten years later (13 March 2014) www.darpa.mil/news-events/2014-03-13

23 T Lewis (25 October 2015) Tony Fadell: The man who wants to take control of your home. www.theguardian.com/technology/2015/oct/25/tony-fadell-nest-labs-smart-thermostats-smoke-alarms

24 AK (21 July 2009) I, for one, welcome our new insect overlords. http://knowyourmeme.com/memes/i-for-one-welcome-our-new-insect-overlords

25 D Muoio (10 March 2016) Why Go is so much harder for AI to beat than chess. www.businessinsider.com/why-google-ai-game-go-is-harder-than-chess-2016-3

26 T S Noam Brown (17 December 2017) Superhuman AI for heads-up no-limit poker: Libratus beats top professionals. http://science.sciencemag.org/content/early/2017/12/15/science.aao1733.full

27 What is narrow, general and super artifical intelligence (12 May 2017) https://bdtechtalks.com/2017/05/12/what-is-narrow-general-and-super-artificial-intelligence

28 G Narula (1 March 2018) Examples of artificial intelligence: Work and school. www.techemergence.com/everyday-examples-of-ai

29 What is machine learning? A definition (no date). www.expertsystem.com/machine-learning-definition

30 C Shu (no date) Waze signs data-sharing deal with AI-based traffic management startup Waycare. https://techcrunch.com/2018/04/26/waze-signs-data-sharing-deal-with-ai-based-traffic-management-startup-waycare/

31 J Brownlee (16 August 2016) What is deep learning? https://machinelearningmastery.com/what-is-deep-learning

32 M Nielsen (2018) Using neural nets to recognize handwritten digits. http://neuralnetworksanddeeplearning.com/chap1.html

33 M Kiser (11 August 2016) Introduction to natural
    language processing (NLP). https://blog.algorithmia.com/
    introduction-natural-language-processing-nlp

34 D Amerland (10 October 2017) Computer vision and
    why it is so difficult. https://towardsdatascience.com/
    computer-vision-and-why-it-is-so-difficult-1ed55e0d65be

35 One vision. Your safety (no date). https://www.mobileye.com/en-us

36 A Gibson and J Patterson (2016) *Deep Learning*, O'Reilly Media

37 www.alivecor.com

38 www.happitech.com

39 B Marr (25 January 2018) Why the internet of medical things
    (IoMT) will start to transform healthcare in 2018. www.forbes.com/
    sites/bernardmarr/2018/01/25/why-the-internet-of-medical-things-
    iomt-will-start-to-transform-healthcare-in-2018/#323523b84a3c

40 S Khoshafian (19 January 2018) Digital transformation of
    healthcare: IoMT connectivity, AI, and value streams. https://
    theiotmagazine.com/digital-transformation-of-healthcare-iomt-
    connectivity-ai-and-value-streams-62edc0f2be1a

41 T Perdue (7 July 2017) Applications of augmented reality.
    www.lifewire.com/applications-of-augmented-reality-2495561

42 A Pardes (20 September 2017) Ikea's new app flaunts
    what you'll love most about AR. www.wired.com/story/
    ikea-place-ar-kit-augmented-reality

43 Z M Angela Li (1 March 2011) Virtual reality and pain
    management: current trends and future directions.
    www.ncbi.nlm.nih.gov/pmc/articles/PMC3138477

44 C T Loguidice (5 September 2017) Virtual reality
    for pain management: A weapon against the opioid
    epidemic? www.clinicalpainadvisor.com/painweek-2017/
    chronic-pain-management-with-virtual-reality/article/684461

45 K Sennaar (16 November 2017) Artificial intelligence
    for energy efficiency and renewable energy:
    6 current applications. www.techemergence.com/
    artificial-intelligence-for-energy-efficiency-and-renewable-energy

46 A Chowdhry (8 October 2013) What can 3D printing
do? Here are 6 creative examples www.forbes.com/sites/
amitchowdhry/2013/10/08/what-can-3d-printing-do-here-are-6-
creative-examples/#5e1550fc5491

47 www.makerbot.com

48 A Richardot (10 August 2017) How 3D printing can help build
artificial intelligence. www.sculpteo.com/blog/2017/08/10/
how-3d-printing-can-help-build-artificial-intelligence

49 Quantum computing (no date). https://dwavefederal.com/system

50 O Oksman (11 June 2016) How nanotechnology
research could cure cancer and other diseases.
www.theguardian.com/lifeandstyle/2016/jun/11/
nanotechnology-research-potential-cure-cancer-genetic-level

51 F Diana (19 August 2016) Artificial intelligence intersects
with nanotechnology. https://medium.com/@frankdiana/
artificial-intelligence-intersects-with-nanotechnology-
a674204daa31

52 K Saarikivi (no date) The rise of empathy-enabling technology.
www.reaktor.com/blog/the-rise-of-empathy-enabling-technology

Chapter 6: The SUPER Framework

1 G Dobush (23 October 2017) Bon voyage, captain (and crew):
The first self-driving ships will soon set sail. https://medium.com/
cxo-magazine/bon-voyage-captain-and-crew-the-first-self-driving-
ships-will-soon-set-sail-78bf5c0b4960

2 W Knight (23 May 2017) Curiosity may be vital for
truly smart AI. www.technologyreview.com/s/607886/
curiosity-may-be-vital-for-truly-smart-ai/

3 J Ogden (24 March 2017) Artificial intelligence could speed airport
security. http://jetsettershomestead.boardingarea.com/2017/03/24/
artificial-intelligence-speed-airport-security-screening/#sthash.
hksB3jFM.dpbs

4 BP Malcolm Frank (12 June 2017) What Netflix teaches us about using AI to create amazing customer experiences. www.mycustomer.com/service/channels/what-netflix-teaches-us-about-using-ai-to-create-amazing-customer-experiences

5 AI technology automatically records soccer matches (31 August 2017) https://news.developer.nvidia.com/ai-technology-automatically-records-soccer-matches/

6 K Sennaar (2 March 2018) Artificial intelligence in sports: Current and future applications. www.techemergence.com/artificial-intelligence-in-sports/

7 A Dave (24 August 2017) How Ai protects PayPal's payments and performance. https://blogs.nvidia.com/blog/2017/08/24/how-ai-protects-paypals-payments-and-performance/

8 M Cassidy (30 December 2014) Centaur chess shows power of teaming human and machine. www.huffingtonpost.com/mike-cassidy/centaur-chess-shows-power_b_6383606.html

9 What is collective intelligence and why should you use it? (no date). www.getsmarter.com/career-advice/industry-advice/collective-intelligence

10 T Malone (21 November 2012) Collective intelligence: A conversation with Thomas M. Malone. www.edge.org/conversation/thomas_w__malone-collective-intelligence

11 D DeMuro (January 2018) 7 best semi-autonomous systems available right now. www.autotrader.com/best-cars/7-best-semi-autonomous-systems-available-right-now-271865

12 Watson Virtual Agent (no date). www.ibm.com/us-en/marketplace/cognitive-customer-engagement

13 T Kontzer (27 January 2017) KLM customer service reps avoid turbulence in social media with AI tool, https://blogs.nvidia.com/blog/2017/01/27/faster-customer-service-with-ai/

14 W Oremus (3 January 2016) Who controls your Facebook feed. www.slate.com/articles/technology/cover_story/2016/01/how_facebook_s_news_feed_algorithm_works.html

15 T Taylor (20 January 2016) Football coaches are turning to AI for help calling plays. www.wired.com/2016/01/ football-coaches-are-turning-to-ai-for-help-calling-plays

16 A Solomon (7 April 2017) A new smart technology will help cities drastically reduce their traffic congestion. www.pastemagazine.com/articles/2017/04/a-new-smart-technology-will-help-cities-drasticall.html

17 K Sennaar (18 February 2018) How the 4 largest airlines use artificial intelligence. www.techemergence.com/ airlines-use-artificial-intelligence

18 P Arntz (9 March 2018) How artificial intelligence and machine learning will impact cybersecurity. https://blog.malwarebytes.com/ security-world/2018/03/how-artificial-intelligence-and-machine-learning-will-impact-cybersecurity

19 ME Porter (1998) *Competitive advantage: Creating and sustaining superior performance,* Free Press

20 B Snyder (6 June 2015) 9 facts about Walmart that will surprise you. http://fortune.com/2015/06/06/walmart-facts

21 J Dudovskiy (1 Septmber 2016) IKEA business strategy and competitive advantage: Capitalising on IKEA concept. https:// research-methodology.net/ikea-business-strategy-competitive-advantage-capitalising-ikea-concept/

22 B Marr (29 August 2017) How Walmart is using machine learning AI, IoT and big data to boost retail performance. www.forbes.com/sites/bernardmarr/2017/08/29/how-walmart-is-using-machine-learning-ai-iot-and-big-data-to-boost-retail-performance/

23 S Meredith (26 January 2018) Ikea sees 'massive opportunities' with artificial intelligence and virtual reality. www.cnbc. com/2018/01/26/ikea-sees-massive-opportunities-with-artificial-intelligence-and-virtual-reality.html

24 H Reese (no date) Elon Musk and the cult of Tesla: How a tech startup rattled the auto industry to its core. www.techrepublic.com/article/elon-musk-and-the-cult-of-tesla-how-a-tech-startup-rattled-the-auto-industry-to-its-core/

25 Understainding manufacturing tiers (no date). www.ever-roll.com/ understanding-manufacturing-tiers/

26 www.harley-davidson.com/us/en/about-us/company.html

Chapter 7: Speed

1 T S Helen Mayhew (October 2016) Making data analytics work for you – instead of the other way around. www.mckinsey.com/ business-functions/digital-mckinsey/our-insights/making-data-analytics-work-for-you-instead-of-the-other-way-around

2 Fractal Foundation (no date) What is chaos theory? https:// fractalfoundation.org/resources/what-is-chaos-theory

3 Ford's assembly line starts rolling (no date) www.history.com/ this-day-in-history/fords-assembly-line-starts-rolling

4 J K-C Wu (15 October 2000) Japanese automakers, U.S. suppliers and supply-chain superiority. https://sloanreview.mit.edu/ article/japanese-automakers-us-suppliers-and-supplychain-superiority

5 The American aerospace industry during World War II (no date). www.centennialofflight.net/essay/Aerospace/WWII_Industry/Aero7.htm

6 T Oppong (22 August 2017) The Kaizen approach to achieving your biggest goal (The philosophy of constant improvement). https://medium.com/the-mission/the-kaizen-approach-to-achieving-your-biggest-goal-the-philosophy-of-constant-improvement-172033f8346

7 What is agile? What is scrum? (no date). www.cprime.com/ resources/what-is-agile-what-is-scrum

8 Agile 101 (no date). www.agilealliance.org/agile101

9 What is scrum? (no date). www.scrum.org/resources/what-is-scrum

10 www.mooreslaw.org

11 Adobe Sensei (no date). www.adobe.com/sensei.html

12 M Techlabs (7 February 2018) How will AI-powered customer service help customer support agents? https://chatbotsmagazine. com/how-will-artificial-intelligence-powered-customer-service-help-customer-support-agents-4fc9054a6a6b

13 D Khmelnitskaya (19 February 2018) 6 best ai chatbots to improve your customer service. www.livechatinc.com/blog/ chatbots-improve-customer-service

14 J Hitch (6 October 2017) Smart(er) manufacturing: How AI is changing the industry. www.newequipment.com/plant-operations/ smarter-manufacturing-how-ai-changing-industry

15 J Walker (24 August 2017) Machine learning in manufacturing: Present and future use-cases. www.techemergence.com/ machine-learning-in-manufacturing

16 DR Busch (2 March 2018) Artificial intelligence: Optimizing industrial operations. www.siemens.com/innovation/en/home/ pictures-of-the-future/industry-and-automation/the-future-of-manufacturing-ai-in-industry.html

17 L Fast (26 March 2018) What role will big data analytics and AI play in the future of lean manufacturing? www.industryweek.com/ operations/what-role-will-big-data-analytics-and-ai-play-future-lean-manufacturing

18 E Waltz (5 April 2017) IBM, Intel, Stanford bet on AI to speed up disease diagnosis and drug discovery. https://spectrum.ieee.org/ the-human-os/biomedical/diagnostics/ibm-intel-stanford-bet-on-ai-to-speed-up-disease-diagnosis-and-drug-discovery

19 B Siwicki (3 December 2017) Future-proofing AI: Embrace machine learning now because healthcare adoption is picking up speed. www.healthcareitnews.com/news/ future-proofing-ai-embrace-machine-learning-now-because-healthcare-adoption-picking-speed

20 How to speed up your checkout process and reduce customer wait times (19 May 2016). https://insights.moneris. com/h/i/254800068-how-to-speed-up-your-checkout-process-and-reduce-customer-wait-times

21 M Harris (26 October 2016) AI-powered body scanners
    could soon be inspecting you in public places. www.theguar
    dian.com/technology/2016/oct/25/
    airport-body-scanner-artificial-intelligence

22 J Beckett (25 January 2017) Getting out of line: AI lets
    shoppers avoid long waits at checkout. https://blogs.nvidia.com/
    blog/2017/01/25/ai-end-checkout-lines

23 E Brown (28 November 2017) AI: The ultimate personal shopper?
    www.zdnet.com/article/ai-the-ultimate-personal-shopper

24 D Kirkpatrick (23 May 2017) Report: 45% of retailers expect
    to use AI within 3 years. www.marketingdive.com/news/
    report-45-of-retailers-expect-to-use-ai-within-3-years/443320

25 E Brown (28 November 2017) AI: The ultimate personal shopper?
    www.zdnet.com/article/ai-the-ultimate-personal-shopper

Chapter 8: Understanding

1 Axiom Zen (10 January 2018) What most people don't understand
   about AI and the the state of machine learning. https://medium.
   com/axiomzenteam/what-most-people-dont-understand-about-ai-
   and-the-the-state-of-machine-learning-ed007a987108

2 AI machine learning to drive 'real time bid'
   advertising spend to $42bn globally by 2021
   (5 September 2016). https://martechtoday.com/
   value-applying-artificial-intelligence-display-advertising-199306

3 J Kressmann (8 February 2017) The value of applying artificial
   intelligence in display advertising. www.emarketer.com/Article/
   How-Businesses-Preparing-Artificial-Intelligence/1015193

4 A Grow (9 June 2017) The value of applying artificial
   intelligence in display advertising. https://martechtoday.com/
   value-applying-artificial-intelligence-display-advertising-199306

5 http://modiface.com

6   M Palin (21 October 2017) Houses of the future: Smart mirrors, medical testing toilets, virtual closets. www.news.com.au/technology/innovation/design/houses-of-the-future-smart-mirrors-medical-testing-toilets-virtual-closets/news-story/8d31f354ec6ed5f094568fff50ecc096

7   ibid.

8   S Shea (October 2017) Smart home or building. http://internetofthingsagenda.techtarget.com/definition/smart-home-or-building

9   E Winick (7 November 2017) Every spreadsheet has a narrative to tell – just add some AI. www.technologyreview.com/s/609368/every-spreadsheet-has-a-narrative-to-tell-just-add-some-ai

10 Turn your data into better decisions with Quill (no date). https://narrativescience.com/Platform

11 C Ghai (18 October 2016) Narrative Science's Chetan Ghai gives insight to how an AI-powered business works. https://aibusiness.com/narrative-sciences-chetan-ghai-gives-insight-to-how-an-ai-powered-business-works

12 D Woods (31 August 2016) Data-driven storytelling and dashboards: How Narrative Science's NLG reaches a new level. www.forbes.com/sites/danwoods/2016/08/31/data-driven-storytelling-and-dashboards-how-narrative-sciences-nlg-reaches-a-new-level/#49fe6e317e98

13 Adobe Experience Cloud (no date). www.adobe.com/experience-cloud.html

14 S Harper (19 April 2017) Ada is an AI-powered doctor app and telemedicine service. https://techcrunch.com/2017/04/19/ada-health

15 Ada – personal health companion (15 June 2017) www.appsunveiled.com/ada-personal-health-companion

16 AI glasses – 'know you again' (2017) Cannes Lions International Festival of Creativity 2017. www.adforum.com/award-organization/6650183/showcase/2017/ad/34546746

17 The way the brain buys (18 December 2008) www.economist.com/node/12792420

Chapter 9: Performance

1 Introduction to key performance indicators (no date). www.klipfolio.com/resources/kpi-examples

2 S Tzu. *The Art of War*

3 G Spencer (17 September 2017) Artificial intelligence and Formula One: Bots on pole position in the race for technology. https://news. microsoft.com/apac/features/artificial-intelligence-formula-one-bots-pole-position-race-technology

4 Artificial intelligence in Formula 1 strategy: Part 1/2 (no date). www.artificial-intelligence.blog/news/ artificial-intelligence-in-formula-1-strategy-part-1-of-2

5 G Spencer (17 September 2017) Artificial intelligence and Formula One: Bots on pole position in the race for technology. https://news. microsoft.com/apac/features/artificial-intelligence-formula-one-bots-pole-position-race-technology

6 D Sarkar (23 September 2017) Microsoft HoloLens: Renault Sport CIO shares how Formula One can use it. www.news18.com/news/ tech/microsoft-hololens-renault-sport-cio-shares-how-formula-one-can-use-it-1525967.html

7 V Highfield (1 March 2018) Microsoft HoloLens: Everything you'll ever need to know about Microsoft's AR device. www. expertreviews.co.uk/microsoft/microsoft-hololens

8 D Faggella (1 Feburary 2018) Artificial intelligence in retail: 10 present and future use cases. www.techemergence.com/ artificial-intelligence-retail

9 TS Helen Mayhew (October 2016) Making data analytics work for you – instead of the other way around. www.mckinsey.com/ business-functions/digital-mckinsey/our-insights/making-data-analytics-work-for-you-instead-of-the-other-way-around

10 Where does your data come from? (no date). www.reachmarketing. com/where-does-your-data-come-from/

11 M Yao (27 October 2017) Future factories: How AI
    enables smart manufacturing. https://medium.com/topbots/
    future-factories-how-ai-enables-smart-manufacturing-c1405f4ec0e6

12 ibid.

13 R Barrat (10 October 2016) How automation is changing the
    supply chain, www.sdcexec.com/warehousing/article/12267524/
    how-automation-is-changing-the-supply-chain

14 P Dorfman (3 January 2018) 3 advances changing the future
    of artificial intelligence in manufacturing. www.autodesk.com/
    redshift/future-of-artificial-intelligence

15 E Ackerman (20 November 2017) iRobot testing software to make
    sense of all rooms in a house. https://spectrum.ieee.org/automaton/
    robotics/home-robots/how-irobots-roomba-will-roomify-your-home

16 Can artificial intelligence help improve agricultural
    productivity? (19 December 2017) www.e-agriculture.org/news/
    can-artificial-intelligence-help-improve-agricultural-productivity

17 K Sato (31 August 2016) How a Japanese cucumber farmer is
    using deep learning and TensorFlow. https://cloud.google.com/blog/
    big-data/2016/08/how-a-japanese-cucumber-farmer-is-using-deep-
    learning-and-tensorflow

18 S Askew (9 January 2018) Artificial intelligence will transform the
    global logistics network in three key areas. www.inboundlogistics.
    com/cms/article/ai-to-transform-global-logistics-in-three-ways

19 How AI is going to shape the future of shipping and logistics
    (no date). http://primaryfreight.com/blog/index.php/2017/12/07/
    how-ai-is-going-to-shape-the-future-of-shipping-and-logistics

20 ibid.

21 O Pickup (2 February 2018) What happens inside Rolls-Royce R2
    Data Labs? www.telegraph.co.uk/education/stem-awards/digital/
    r2-data-lab

22 E Biba (14 February 2017) The jet engine with 'digital twins'. www.bbc.com/autos/story/20170214-how-jet-engines-are-made

23 ibid.

Chapter 10: Experimentation

1 I Rodà (November/December 2016) Aqueducts: Quenching Rome's thirst. www.nationalgeographic.com/archaeology-and-history/ magazine/2016/11-12/roman-aqueducts-engineering-innovation

2 D Szondy (24 January 2018) Falcon heavy vs. the classic Saturn V. https://newatlas.com/falcon-heavy-saturn-v/53090

3 ibid.

4 T Fernholz (21 February 2017) SpaceX's self-landing rocket is a flying robot that's great at math. https://qz.com/915702/ the-spacex-falcon-9-rocket-you-see-landing-on-earth-is-really-a-sophisticated-flying-robot

5 BT Tomas Chamorro-Premuzic (5 July 2017) Can AI ever be as curious as humans? https://hbr.org/2017/04/can-ai-ever-be-as-curious-as-humans

6 T Ward (24 May 2017) Naturally curious. https://disruptionhub. com/creativity-and-ai

7 J Vincent (21 July 2016) Google uses DeepMind AI to cut data center energy bills. www.theverge.com/2016/7/21/12246258/ google-deepmind-ai-data-center-cooling

8 A Ng (March 2018) How artificial intelligence and data add value to businesses. www.mckinsey. com/global-themes/artificial-intelligence/ how-artificial-intelligence-and-data-add-value-to-businesses

9 J Brownlee (16 March 2016) Supervised and unsupervised machine learning algorithms. https://machinelearningmastery.com/ supervised-and-unsupervised-machine-learning-algorithms

10 N Castle (2 February 2018) What is semi-supervised learning? www.datascience.com/blog/what-is-semi-supervised-learning

11 A Ng (March 2018) How artificial intelligence and data add value to businesses. www.mckinsey.com/global-themes/artificial-intelligence/how-artificial-intelligence-and-data-add-value-to-businesses

12 M Zhang (21 October 2017) Adobe Scene Stitch is like content-aware fill with an imagination. https://petapixel.com/2017/10/21/adobe-scene-stitch-like-content-aware-fill-imagination

Chapter 11: Results

1 L Columbus (16 October 2017) 80% of enterprises are investing in AI today. www.forbes.com/sites/louiscolumbus/2017/10/16/80-of-enterprises-are-investing-in-ai-today/#7ea8f2324d8e

2 W Knight (16 September 2015) The Roomba now sees and maps a home. www.technologyreview.com/s/541326/the-roomba-now-sees-and-maps-a-home

3 S Buhr (14 May 2017) RoboWaiter wants to make American restaurants great again with robots. https://techcrunch.com/2017/05/14/robowaiter-wants-to-make-american-restaurants-great-again-with-robots

4 S Lay (13 November 2015) Uncanny valley: Why we find human-like robots and dolls so creepy. www.theguardian.com/commentisfree/2015/nov/13/robots-human-uncanny-valley

5 Zebra Medical Vision (no date) https://us.zebra-med.com

6 24/7 Staff (29 September 2016) Transforming logistics with artificial intelligence. www.supplychain247.com/article/transforming_logistics_with_artificial_intelligence

7 Scott Amyx (10 October 2017) Here's how AI benefits companies. https://scottamyx.com/2017/10/10/companies-benefit-artificialintelligence

8 Teradata (11 October 2017) State of artificial intelligence for enterprises. www.teradata.com

9 L Columbus (22 June 2017) Artificial intelligence will enable 38% profit gains by 2035. www.forbes.com/sites/louiscolumbus/2017/06/22/artificial-intelligence-will-enable-38-profit-gains-by-2035/#5bb7110b1969

10 Z Hedge (13 October 2017) AI-powered chatbots to drive dramatic cost savings in healthcare. saving $3.6 billion by 2022. www.iot-now.com/2017/10/13/69037-ai-powered-chatbots-drive-dramatic-cost-savings-healthcare-saving-3-6-billion-2022

11 D Hauss (1 August 2017) ROI of AI: 5 ways retailers are embracing the innovation. www.retailtouchpoints.com/features/trend-watch/roi-of-ai-5-ways-retailers-are-embracing-the-innovation

12 M Knickrehm, B Berthon and P Daugherty (2016) *Digital disruption: The growth multiplier*, Accenture. www.accenture.com/t00010101T000000__w__/br-pt/_acnmedia/PDF-14/Accenture-Strategy-Digital-Disruption-Growth-Multiplier-Brazil.pdf

13 D Newman (16 February 2017) Innovation vs. transformation: The difference in a digital world. www.forbes.com/sites/danielnewman/2017/02/16/innovation-vs-transformation-the-difference-in-a-digital-world/#3464983b65e8

Chapter 12: Where to start

1 www.businessdictionary.com/definition/silo-mentality.html

2 A Rao (5 March 2014) The 5 dimensions of the so-called data scientist. http://usblogs.pwc.com/emerging-technology/the-5-dimensions-of-the-so-called-data-scientist

3 R Willcox (27 July 2017) You need to assemble a crack AI team: Where do you even start? www.theregister.co.uk/2017/07/27/assembling_an_ai_team

4 AD Farri (15 January 2018) The 5 things your AI unit needs to do. https://hbr.org/2018/01/the-5-things-your-ai-unit-needs-to-do

5   Altesoft (10 May 2017) How to structure a data science team: Key models and roles to consider. www.altexsoft.com/blog/datascience/ how-to-structure-data-science-team-key-models-and-roles

6   Smartsheet (no date) What's the difference? Agile vs scrum vs waterfall vs kanban. www.smartsheet.com/ agile-vs-scrum-vs-waterfall-vs-kanban

7   ibid.

8   ibid.

9   ibid.

10   What's the difference between programmatic and RTB? (no date). www.studybreakmedia.com/whats-difference-programmatic-rtb

11   Microsoft (no date). Cognitive Services. https://azure.microsoft. com/en-us/services/cognitive-services

12   Adobe Sensei (no date). www.adobe.com/sensei.html

Chapter 13: Security, privacy and ethics

1   T George (11 January 2017) The role of artificial intelligence in cyber security. www.securityweek.com/ role-artificial-intelligence-cyber-security

2   R Kh (no date) How AI is the future of cybersecurity. www.infosecurity-magazine.com/next-gen-infosec/ai-future- cybersecurity

3   ibid.

4   M Krigsman (18 June 2017) Artificial intelligence and privacy engineering: Why it matters NOW. www.zdnet.com/article/ artificial-intelligence-and-privacy-engineering-why-it-matters-now

5   S Touw (May 2017) Anonymization and the future of data science. www.kdnuggets.com/2017/04/anonymization-future-data-science.html

6   G McCord (2015) What you should know about 'anonymous' aggregate data about you. https://chooseprivacyweek.org/ choose-privacy-week-2015-what-you-should-know-about- anonymous-aggregate-data-about-you

7 J Spacey (10 November 2016) 4 types of data anonymization. https://simplicable.com/new/data-anonymization

8 C Williamson (5 January 2017) Pseudonymization vs anonymization and how they help with GDPR. www.protegrity. com/pseudonymization-vs-anonymization-help-gdpr/

9 RSA (2017) RSA privacy and security report. www.rsa.com/ content/dam/en/e-book/rsa-data-privacy-report.pdf

10 M Nadeau (16 February 2018) General Data Protection Regulation (GDPR) requirements, deadlines and facts. www.csoonline. com/article/3202771/data-protection/general-data-protection-regulation-gdpr-requirements-deadlines-and-facts.html

11 GDPR EU.org (no date). Fines and penalities. www.gdpreu.org/ compliance/fines-and-penalties

12 California Department of Health Care Services (no date). Health Insurance Portability and Accountability Act. www.dhcs.ca.gov/ formsandpubs/laws/hipaa/Pages/1.00WhatisHIPAA.aspx

13 Asilomar AI principles (no date). https://futureoflife.org/ ai-principles

14 J Bossmann (21 October 2016) Top 9 ethical issues in artificial intelligence. www.weforum.org/agenda/2016/10/ top-10-ethical-issues-in-artificial-intelligence

15 BV Toness (4 April 2017) Five questions for David Autor. https:// undark.org/article/five-questions-for-david-autor

16 MIT Sloan School of Management (2017) Artificial intelligence: Implications for business strategy. Nodule 5, unit 2, MIT Sloan School of Management

Chapter 14: Yesterday, tomorrow and today

1 A C Clarke (1951) 'Sentinel of Eternity', *Ten Story Fantasy* magazine; (1968) *2001: A Space Odyssey*, New American Library

2 I Azimov (1956) *I, Robot*, Signet

3 D Gerrold (1972) *When HARLIE Was One,* Ballantine Books

4 T J Ryan (1977) *The Adolescence of P-1,* Macmillan Publishing

5 P Baines (2010) *Alpha Redemption,* Splashdown Books

6 PK Dick (1968) *Do Androids Dream of Electric Sheep?* Ballantine Books

7 M Rouse (July 2017) Smart city. https://internetofthingsagenda. techtarget.com/definition/smart-city

8 N Windpassinger (2017) Internet of things: Digitize or die. IoT Hub

9 A Dhanalakshmi, P Lathapriya and K Divya (March 2017) A smart helmet for improving safety in mining industry. www.scribd.com/ document/343713928/A-Smart-Helmet-for-Improving-Safety-in-Mining-Industry

10 DZ Morris (22 July 2017) World's first autonomous ship to launch in 2018. http://fortune.com/2017/07/22/ first-autonomous-ship-yara-birkeland

11 Marex (27 August 2017) The autonomous revolution. www.maritime-executive.com/features/the-autonomous-revolution#gs._x8q2kA

Chapter 15: Next-Gen Creativity

1 L FridMan (no date). *Artificial Intelligence Podcast.* MIT Lex FridMan: https://lexfridman.com/ai/

2 G Wolf (1998, February 1) *Steve Jobs: The Next Insanely Great Thing.* www.wired.com/1996/02/jobs-2

3 D Eagleman (2017) *The Runaway Species: How human creativity remakes the world.* Catapult

4 C M Christensen (2011) *The Innovator's Dilemma: The Revolutionary Book that Will Change the Way You Do Business.* HarperBusiness.

5 McKinsey (no date). *The Business Value of Design.* McKinsey.

6 Pfeiffer Report (2018) *Creativity and technology.*

7 Artificial Intelligence Wiki (no date). *A Beginner's Guide to Generative Adversarial Networks (GANs).* Retrieved from Artificial Intelligence Wiki: https://skymind.ai/wiki/generative-adversarial-network-gan

8 J Hui (22 June 2018) *GAN – Some cool applications of GANs.* Medium. https://medium.com/@jonathan_hui/gan-some-cool-applications-of-gans-4c9ecca35900

9 Z Thoutt (26 September 2017) *What are Creative Adversarial Networks (CANs)?* Medium. https://hackernoon.com/what-are-creative-adversarial-networks-cans-bb81d09aa235

10 A Missinato (14 February 2018) *Is creative writing still a human prerogative?* Spindox Digital Soul. www.spindox.it/en/blog/ai-deep-writing

11 Whitney Museum of American Art (no date). *Andy Warhol – From A to B and Back Again Nov 12, 2018-Mar 31, 2019.* https://whitney.org/Exhibitions/AndyWarhol

12 D&AD (no date). *How A.I. and Machine Learning Will Change Design and the Creative Industries in 2018.* www.dandad.org/en/d-ad-benjamin-hubert-industrial-design-creativity-technology-features-opinions

13 T Greene (15 June 2018) *Researchers developed an AI to detect DeepFakes.* https://thenextweb.com/artificial-intelligence/2018/06/15/researchers-developed-an-ai-to-detect-deepfakes

Index

CPSIA information can be obtained
at www.ICGtesting.com
Printed in the USA
BVHW021802130120
569380BV00017B/619/P

9 780749 483838